THE LAST SHALL BE THE FIRST

THE EAST EUROPEAN FINANCIAL CRISIS, 2008–10

Anders Åslund

PETERSON INSTITUTE FOR INTERNATIONAL ECONOMICS

Washington, DC

October 2010

Anders Åslund, known to repeatedly challenge conventional wisdom on "transition economies," is a leading specialist on postcommunist economic transformation with more than 30 years of experience in the field. He boldly predicted the fall of the Soviet Union in his Gorbachev's Struggle for Economic Reform (1989). In How Russia Became a Market Economy (1995) he firmly stated that the only choice Russia had was market reform.

This is Dr. Åslund's tenth book. His recent books are How Ukraine Became a Market Economy and Democracy (2009), Russia's Capitalist Revolution (2007), and How Capitalism Was Built: The Transformation of the Central and Eastern Europe, Russia, and Central Asia (2007). He has edited fourteen books, most recently Russia after the Global Economic Crisis (2010) and The Russia Balance Sheet (2009). He has also published widely, including in Foreign Affairs, Foreign Policy, National Interest, New York Times, Washington Post, Financial Times, and Wall Street Journal.

Dr Åslund joined the Peterson Institute for International Economics as senior fellow in January 2006. Previously, he served as a Swedish diplomat in Kuwait, Geneva, Poland, Moscow, and Stockholm. From 1989 until 1994, he was professor and founding director of the Stockholm Institute of Transition Economics at the Stockholm School of Economics. Dr. Åslund has also been a scholar at the Kennan Institute for Advanced Russian Studies, Woodrow Wilson International Center for Scholars, the Brookings Institution and at the Carnegie Endowment for International Peace, where he was a senior associate, director of the Russian and Eurasian Program, and co-directed the program on post-Soviet economies at the Carnegie Moscow Center. He is co-chairman of the Board of Trustees of the Kyiv School of Economics and chairman of the Advisory Council of the Center for Social and Economic Research (CASE), Warsaw.

PETER G. PETERSON INSTITUTE FOR INTERNATIONAL ECONOMICS
1750 Massachusetts Avenue, NW
Washington, DC 20036-1903
(202) 328-9000   FAX: (202) 659-3225
www.piie.com

C. Fred Bergsten, *Director*
Edward A. Tureen, *Director of Publications, Marketing, and Web Development*

Figures by BMWW
Printing by United Book Press, Inc
Cover design by Peggy Archambault
Cover photo: © Jon Hicks/Corbis

Printed in the United States of America

12   11   10   5   4   3   2   1

Library of Congress Cataloging-in-Publication Data

Åslund, Anders, 1952-
  The last shall be the first : the East European financial crisis, 2008-10 / Anders Aslund.
     p. cm.
  ISBN 978-0-88132-521-8
  1. Financial crises—Europe, Eastern. 2. Europe, Eastern—Economic policy. 3. Banks and banking--Europe, Eastern. I. Title.

HB3782.9.A84 2010
330.9470009'0511--dc22

                              2010034683

To
Victor & Elena Pinchuk

Contents

Box

Preface

In the fall of 2008, Eastern Europe was the most overheated region in the world economy. When the global financial crisis hit, some of these economies suffered greatly and registered the largest declines in output in 2009. For the Peterson Institute for International Economics, it was natural to devote attention to this crisis. Its causes were obvious, but how was it resolved? In this study, Senior Fellow Anders Åslund draws lessons from the East European financial crisis of 2008–10. This study is brief for the fortuitous reason that the crisis resolution has been so successful. In the second half of 2010, the whole region is likely to have returned to economic growth. Åslund focuses on the ten new eastern members of the European Union.

The greatest surprise is that the worst hit countries—Latvia, Lithuania, and Estonia—were not forced to devalue contrary to claims of a broad chorus of American economists. Instead, these three Baltic countries pursued what they called "internal devaluation." Their governments cut public wages by up to 35 percent, and the private sector followed suit. They slashed public expenditures, and their cost levels became competitive, allowing them to turn their large current account deficits swiftly to substantial surpluses.

Equally amazing was the political economy of this crisis. Instead of widely predicted social unrest, the East European public has accepted their considerable hardship with minimal protests. Åslund argues that multiple factors contributed to social peace. Large majorities favored wages cuts over devaluation as the lesser evil, because the benefits of devaluations would mainly accrue to wealthy exporters. After many years of high economic growth, people were prepared for some suffering. These states had recently become free and were prepared to stand up for their nations, and they were all used to crisis from the postcommunist transition.

Most of the 10 countries in this study changed governments during the financial crisis and some of them did so twice. By and large, the new governments were more determined and competent in their crisis policies, showing that frequent government changes were beneficial for crisis resolution. The most successful governments were coalition governments of several parties, while the only country with majority governments was Hungary, which arguably pursued the worst macroeconomic policies before and after the crisis. These observations suggest a positive reassessment of parliamentary systems leading to coalition governments for the handling of crises.

The International Monetary Fund (IMF) stands out as the great victor on the international stage from the East European financial crisis, but only three countries needed its standby programs. The IMF returned to the old Washington Consensus of a few rudimentary financial conditions, such as tenable exchange rate policy and reasonable fiscal and monetary policy. It allowed these well-governed countries larger public deficits during the crisis and offered much more financing than before with the understanding that this was a temporary current account crisis. The IMF acted even faster than usual.

The European Commission entered into an astonishingly successful partnership with the IMF in Eastern Europe. It allowed the IMF to take the lead, while the Commission provided substantial financing, more than the IMF in the case of Latvia, and checked the work of the IMF. When financial crisis hit the eurozone, however, the European Union seemed to have forgotten all its fortuitous lessons from Eastern Europe, attempting to keep the IMF out. In the end, the European Union came to its senses and let the IMF take the lead also within the eurozone, which helped mitigate the crisis.

Åslund has few kind words for the European Central Bank (ECB). Its single though great contribution was that it eased money supply to salvage the European banking system in the fall of 2008, also saving subsidiaries of West European banks in Eastern Europe. Before the crisis, however, the ECB ignored the massive overheating in some EU members outside of the eurozone, paying minimal attention to financial stability. While the entry conditions to the eurozone demanded that a country peg its exchange rate to the euro for at least two years, the ECB did nothing to stabilize the economies of these candidate countries. It could have offered swap credits, as the US Federal Reserve did to many emerging-market economies, but refused. One conclusion of this book is that the ECB needs to reconsider its policies outside the eurozone and become more proactive.

In the end, the East European economies appear to have emerged even stronger after this crisis. They have maintained their highly competitive tax systems and further reinforced their competitive edge. The crisis has compelled them to undertake beneficial reforms in their public administration, health care, and education. After economic recovery has boosted their tax revenues again, the East European countries are likely to have better fiscal balances than before the crisis and excel the old EU members both in fiscal and structural policies.

The Peter G. Peterson Institute for International Economics is a private, nonprofit institution for the study and discussion of international economic policy. Its purpose is to analyze important issues in that area and to develop and communicate practical new approaches for dealing with them. The Institute is completely nonpartisan.

The Institute is funded by a highly diversified group of philanthropic foundations, private corporations, and interested individuals. About 35 percent of the Institute's resources in our latest fiscal year was provided by contributors outside the United States. The Victor Pinchuk Foundation and Open Society Institute provided generous funding for this study.

The Institute's Board of Directors bears overall responsibilities for the Institute and gives general guidance and approval to its research program, including the identification of topics that are likely to become important over the medium run (one to three years) and that should be addressed by the Institute. The director, working closely with the staff and outside Advisory Committee, is responsible for the development of particular projects and makes the final decision to publish an individual study.

The Institute hopes that its studies and other activities will contribute to building a stronger foundation for international economic policy around the world. We invite readers of these publications to let us know how they think we can best accomplish this objective.

C. FRED BERGSTEN
Director
August 2010

Acknowledgments

Working at the Peterson Institute for International Economics means being in the midst of the global financial crisis because it has been our permanent theme of discussion. What were the key causes of the crisis? Where were the flashpoints? What has been done to resolve it, and what should be done? My focus is Eastern Europe, and I traveled there repeatedly during the crisis.

Within two years, the East European financial crisis had abated and was overtaken by the novel Greek and South European fiscal crisis. At the end of March 2010, my colleague Adam S. Posen suggested that I write a short book about the East European financial crisis and do so before people forgot that it had existed, as the eurozone crisis had taken over. He also proposed that I model my book on Senior Fellow Michael Mussa's book for the Institute, *Argentina and the Fund: From Triumph to Tragedy* (2002). I have tried to follow his two pieces of advice and transform my various fragments of research into a short book.

I decided to concentrate on the ten new East European members of the European Union: Bulgaria, the Czech Republic, Estonia, Hungary, Latvia, Lithuania, Poland, Romania, Slovakia, and Slovenia. Some were hit hard by the crisis (the three Baltic states, Hungary, and Romania), while others escaped. Exchange rate policy was central: two have the euro, four have currency boards, and four floating exchange rates. Though they are all members of the European Union, they have not quite been considered first-class members, rendering their relationship with the European Union a key question.

In the process of writing this book, I greatly benefited from many useful comments and insights from several colleagues and experts. First and foremost, I would like to thank the kind people who read my rough drafts and provided competent and helpful comments on them: Jeff Anderson, Bas Bakker, C. Fred Bergsten, Marek Dabrowski, Balazs Egert, Paul Gregory, Jens Henriksson, Christoph Rosenberg, and Edwin M. Truman.

At the Peterson Institute, I have benefited from multiple comments from many colleagues, notably C. Fred Bergsten, William R. Cline, Morris Goldstein, Randy Henning, Simon Johnson, Joseph E. Gagnon, Jacob Kirkegaard, Michael Mussa, Marcus Noland, Adam S. Posen, Arvind Subramanian, Edwin M. Truman, and John Williamson. I would like to especially mention a study group at the Institute in which Jeff Anderson, Bas Bakker, C. Fred Bergsten, Per Callesen, William R. Cline, Joseph E. Gagnon, Randy Henning, Yusuke Horiguchi, Jacob Kirkegaard, Michael Mussa, Randal K. Quarles, Christoph B. Rosenberg, Edwin M. Truman, and Steven R. Weisman participated and contributed useful comments. Anna Borshchevskaya offered me excellent research assistance and compiled the necessary statistics.

Traveling around Europe, I met and conversed with many wise people, who provided me with great insights. In particular, I would like to thank Czech President Vaclav Klaus, Estonian President Toomas Hendrik Ilves, former Estonian Prime Minister Mart Laar, Latvian Prime Minister Valdis Dombrovskis, Latvian Finance Minister Einars Repse, Chairman of the Bank of Latvia Ilmars Rimsevics, Lithuanian Prime Minister Andrius Kubilius, former Chairman of the Polish National Bank Leszek Balcerowicz, Dr. Ewa Balcerowicz, Professor Marek Dabrowski, Polish Finance Minister Jacek Rostowski, late Chairman of the Polish National Bank Slawomir Skrzypek, Professor Janos Kornai, late Russian Prime Minister Yegor Gaidar, former Slovak Prime Minister Mikulas Dzurinda, Swedish Minister for Foreign Affairs Carl Bildt, Chairman of the Riksbank Stefan Ingves, Swedish Ambassador to Riga Mats Staffansson, Ambassador Olof Ehrenkrona, Swedish Ministry of Finance Director Åke Törnquist, Chairman of the Norwegian Bank Svein Gjedrem, Member of the Board of the Bank of Finland Seppo Honkapohja, First Deputy Chair of the European Investment Bank Eva Srejber, European Commissioner Olli Rehn, Russian Finance Minister Alexei Kudrin, Ukrainian Prime Minister Yulia Tymoshenko, and Ukrainian Deputy Prime Minister Hryhory Nemyria.

At the International Monetary Fund, I would particularly like to thank Age Bakker, Bas Bakker, Marek Belka, Per Callesen, Mark Griffiths, Jens Henriksson, Alexei Mozhin, Ceyla Pazarbasioglu, Christoph Rosenberg, and Poul Thomsen. I have benefited from other conversations in Washington with US Treasury officials Clay Lowery, Jeffrey Baker, Eric Meyer, and Christopher Smart.

I am grateful to the Peterson Institute's publications team, in particular to Edward Tureen for expediently producing the book, as always to Madona Devasahayam for sensitive and elegant copyediting, and to Susann Luetjen for her artistic talent in production and design.

As always, I appreciate the tolerance of my wife, Anna, and my children, Carl and Marianna, for allowing me my pleasure of reading and writing.

This research has been financed by generous grants from the Victor Pinchuk Foundation and the Open Society Institute.

Needless to say, all the mistakes that remain are my own.

ANDERS ÅSLUND
August 2010

1

Introduction

So the last shall be first, and the first last: for many be called, but few chosen.

—Matthew 20:16

In the fall of 2008, Central and Eastern Europe became one of the flashpoints of the global financial crisis. By March 2010, however, the crisis in that region had more or less abated. Public attention moved from Latvia—the country that suffered the greatest pain in the East European crisis—to the PIGS (Portugal, Italy, Greece, and Spain), in particular to Greece. The issue was no longer why Latvia must devalue but what Greece could learn from Latvia. Soon few will remember there was a crisis in Eastern Europe, because nothing is more easily taken for granted than success.

I realized that I had better write a book quickly to bring home the lessons from this episode before it faded from public memory. What lessons can be drawn from the East European financial crisis for Southern Europe and the rest of the European Union? What happened during the East European financial crisis, and how was it resolved so quickly?

For world output, the East European financial crisis was of minimal significance (see box 1.1 and table 1.1 for the countries I focus on). The three main crisis countries, Hungary, Romania, and Latvia, together accounted for only 2 percent of EU GDP, approximately as much as Greece. The greatest concern was the possible impact of this crisis on the European banking system, but it was also a sign of a global financial system out of balance.

Financial warning bells had been ringing since 2006 because of large current account deficits in many of these countries. A rule of thumb is that a current account deficit of more than 4 to 5 percent of GDP is worrisome, and almost all had larger deficits. Latvia and Bulgaria topped the lot with current account deficits in 2007 of 23 and 25 percent of GDP, respectively. As a consequence, some countries had accumulated large foreign debt.

This could not go on, as many, including the International Monetary Fund (IMF), repeatedly stated.[1]

But alternative interpretations dominated. A lot of capital had moved permanently to these countries. An unusually large share of the current account deficits was financed by foreign direct investment, and much of the remaining capital flow consisted of "related" lending similar to foreign direct investment. When a West European bank acquired a subsidiary in the east, its equity capital was recorded as foreign direct investment, but it added even larger loans, which were registered as short-term bank credit. Yet any West European bank would have been reluctant to withdraw such credits, which would have undermined the value of its core investment.

Marek Dabrowski argued that the current account flows within the euro area or to countries with currency boards soon to join the eurozone should not really be seen as current account deficits:

> In a world of free capital movement the geographic origin of capital has lost its importance, and capital invested abroad does not need to return to the country of "residence." There is no "home country bias" in investment decisions any more; the expected rate of return is the key parameter determining these decisions. Some countries may offer a higher rate of return for a long period of time, becoming persistent capital importers, while others may offer a surplus saving on a sustainable basis.[2]

These were rational capital flows to areas offering higher return on investment. Capital was transferred from inefficient, overtaxed, slow-growing, bureaucratized old Europe to efficient, fast-growing new Europe. Central and Eastern Europe was enjoying far higher growth rates than the EU-15, benefiting from catch-up growth in relation to the still-richer, old EU countries. Moreover, they had lower taxes, fewer social transfers, and more flexible labor markets. Modern neoclassical growth theory states that within similar open-market economies, GDP levels converge over time, leading to the obvious conclusion that European economic convergence would be the natural outcome.[3] For two decades economic convergence had been palpable.[4]

---

1. Morris Goldstein, "Emerging-Market Financial Crises: Lessons and Prospects" (speech, 2007 Annual Meeting, Institute of International Finance, Washington, October 20, 2007); Susan Schadler, "Are Large External Imbalances in Central Europe Sustainable?" in *Challenges of Globalization: Imbalances and Growth*, eds. Anders Åslund and Marek Dabrowski (Washington: Peterson Institute for International Economics, 2008).

2. Marek Dabrowski, "Rethinking Balance of Payments Constraints in a Globalized World" in *Challenges of Globalization: Imbalances and Growth*, eds. Anders Åslund and Marek Dabrowski (Washington: Peterson Institute for International Economics, 2008), 73.

3. Robert J. Barro and Xavier Sala-i-Martin, *Economic Growth* (Cambridge, MA: MIT Press, 2004).

4. Leszek Balcerowicz and Stanley Fischer, eds., *Living Standards and the Wealth of Nations: Successes and Failures in Real Convergence* (Cambridge, MA: MIT Press, 2006).

Box 1.1   The ten Central and East European countries (CEE-10)

In this book, I focus on the ten new eastern members of the European Union: Estonia, Latvia, Lithuania (the three Baltic countries), Poland, the Czech Republic, Slovakia, Hungary, Slovenia (the five Central European countries), Romania, and Bulgaria (Southeastern Europe).[1] Bulgaria and Romania acceded to the European Union in January 2007. The other eight joined in May 2004. Together, I call them the CEE-10 (Central and East European 10), in contrast to the EU-15, the 15 countries that were members of the European Union before 2004.[2] One reason I limit my analysis to these ten countries is that it is difficult to offer a comprehensive narrative on too many different countries with a variety of problems.

The CEE-10 fall conveniently into three groups of countries with regard to exchange rate policy: Slovenia and Slovakia adopted the euro in 2007 and 2009, respectively; Estonia, Latvia, Lithuania, and Bulgaria have fixed exchange rates based on currency boards; and Poland, the Czech Republic, Hungary, and Romania have floating exchange rates and essentially pursue inflation targeting.

Of these ten CEE countries, three—Hungary, Latvia, and Romania—required International Monetary Fund (IMF) standby programs. Further to the east, Belarus, Ukraine, Moldova, Georgia, and Armenia all needed IMF programs, but each had its own set of problems, rendering generalizations difficult; such a large number of countries would cloud any overview. The same is true of the Balkan countries. Another reason for limiting this study to the CEE-10 is that it focuses on the actions of the European Union and the European Central Bank, which played no significant role outside of the European Union. Yet for the sake of context, I mention key events in the broader region.

---

1. The other two new EU members from 2004, Cyprus and Malta, fall outside of this study.

2. The EU-15 are Austria, Belgium, Denmark, Finland, France, Germany, Greece, Ireland, Italy, Luxembourg, the Netherlands, Portugal, Spain, Sweden, and the United Kingdom.

But by 2008, Central and Eastern Europe was in a state of severe overheating in all regards. Inflation surged everywhere and to double digits in Bulgaria, Estonia, Latvia, and Lithuania. Wages and real estate prices skyrocketed, rendering these countries ever less competitive, which further undermined their current account balance. The country with the greatest overexpansion, Latvia, was feeling a credit crunch already in 2007, as its banks seemed overstretched with excessive lending and the risk of a fall in real estate prices with ensuing credit losses was evident.

The big blow was the Lehman Brothers bankruptcy on September 15, 2008. All of a sudden, world liquidity dried up, and vulnerable Eastern Europe was left with no credit. For half a year until the G-20 meeting in

Table 1.1 Overview of the CEE-10 countries

Country	EU member	EMU status	Exchange rate policy	GDP growth (percent annual rate) 2000–07	2009
Baltics					
Estonia	May 2004	ERM II, 2004	Currency board	7.5	−14.1
Latvia	May 2004	ERM II, 2005	Currency board	8.8	−18.4
Lithuania	May 2004	ERM II, 2004	Currency board	8.2	−15.0
Central Europe					
Poland	May 2004		Floating rate	4.1	1.7
Czech Republic	May 2004		Floating rate	4.5	−4.1
Slovakia	May 2004	Euro, January 2009	Euro	5.7	−4.7
Hungary	May 2004		Floating rate	4.0	−6.3
Slovenia	May 2004	Euro, January 2007	Euro	4.4	−7.8
Southeastern Europe					
Bulgaria	January 2007		Currency board	5.5	−5.1
Romania	January 2007		Floating rate	5.6	−7.2

EMU = Economic and Monetary Union
ERM II = European Exchange Rate Mechanism
CPI = consumer price index
IMF = International Monetary Fund

Sources: Eurostat database, http://epp.eurostat.ec.europa.eu; IMF, *World Economic Outlook*, April 2010, www.imf.org.

London on April 2, 2009, global liquidity remained frozen. Private finance could no longer be obtained at any price. The only financing available for countries in need on the edge of the global financial system was government funding, primarily from the IMF.

What Went Wrong and How It Was Fixed

The East European financial crisis was a standard credit boom-and-bust cycle leading to a current account crisis. Large private capital inflows had mounted to too much private debt. Yet leverage in these countries was limited, that is, their credit and money volumes were moderate in relation to their GDP. Still, the pace of their expansion had been dangerously rapid, and increasingly the capital inflows consisted of short-term bank loans, which were spent on consumption and real estate investment. The causes were a combination of three factors: very loose global monetary conditions; an open, attractive investment environment; and exchange rate policies that allowed the global monetary overflow to boost domestic money supply. This was overheating arising from excessive success. Unlike much of Western Europe and the United States, the Central Europeans had not indulged in subprime mortgage loans or collateral debt

Fiscal balance, 2007 (percent of GDP)	Inflation, 2008 (CPI percent)	Current account deficit, 2007 (percent of GDP)	IMF program (type and date)
2.6	10.4	−18.0	
−0.4	15.3	−22.5	Standby, December 2008
−1.0	11.1	−14.6	
−1.9	4.2	−4.0	Flexible credit line, May 2009
−0.6	6.3	−3.1	
−1.9	3.9	−4.8	
−4.9	6.1	−6.4	Standby, October 2008
0.5	5.7	−4.2	
3.5	12.0	−25.4	
−3.1	7.8	−14.4	Standby, March 2009

obligations. Apart from Hungary, none of the Central Europeans suffered from a large fiscal deficit or excessive public debt, and they had no conspicuous systemic flaws.

Exchange rate policy was the dominant policy issue. The ten Central and East European countries (CEE-10) had three different exchange rate regimes. Only two countries, Slovenia and Slovakia, had been allowed by the European Union to adopt the euro in 2007 and 2009, respectively. Four countries had fixed exchange rates based on currency boards—Estonia, Latvia, Lithuania, and Bulgaria. Formally, Latvia did not have a full-fledged currency board, but it operated its financial system as if that were the case. The remaining four countries—Poland, the Czech Republic, Hungary, and Romania—had floating exchange rates and essentially pursued inflation targeting.

The three Baltic countries saw the biggest output plunges of 14 to 18 percent in 2009, and Latvia suffered the deepest financial crisis and needed an IMF program. Countries with the euro or floating exchange rate and decent fiscal policy did well. Poland stood out as the luckiest economy with economic growth in 2009. The Czech Republic, Slovakia, and Slovenia also did reasonably well, while Hungary and Romania required IMF programs, not because of their exchange rate policies but for their comparatively loose fiscal policy.

The four countries that had fixed exchange rates (Bulgaria, Estonia, Latvia, and Lithuania) had no means to sterilize the large capital inflows, as they were caught in the Impossible Trinity: With fixed exchange rates and free capital flows, they could not pursue independent monetary policy. If they had raised their domestic interest rates, they would only have attracted larger capital inflows.[5] They had hardly any bonds. Their only policy tools were fiscal policy and bank regulation, which could and should have been used more, but few did so during the boom. Of the countries with fixed exchange rates, Lithuania and Latvia had almost balanced budgets, while Estonia and Bulgaria displayed steady budget surpluses.

A broad consensus among American economists claimed that all countries with pegged exchange rates would have to devalue, which was their lesson from the East Asian crisis in 1997–98. Also, Russia and Argentina had been forced to devalue. But no single EU country with a fixed exchange rate has devalued, making evident that it was not necessary and perhaps not even desirable. Nor have any of the CEE-10 changed their exchange rate policies. Estonia has been accepted to adopt the euro in January 2011. My personal position throughout—as I elaborate upon below—was that it made no sense for the Baltic countries to devalue.[6]

The severe shock of the international liquidity squeeze from September 2008 caused the floating exchange rates to plummet. In early 2009 worries prevailed that Central and Eastern Europe would suffer a devastating banking crisis, but it never happened. West European banks owned most of the banks in the CEE-10 and the fear was that they would withdraw from the region. In fact, not a single Western bank departed from any country during the crisis. The European Central Bank (ECB) and other central banks in Europe flooded their banks with cheap liquidity, and the European Union stipulated that their banks should not be forced to sell their foreign subsidiaries. The IMF and the European Bank for Reconstruction and Development (EBRD) demanded coordinated commitments from the banks concerned not to cut and run from the east. From April 2009, the credit crunch eased, and the floating exchange rates recovered. In the end, most loans were rolled over and the feared financial withdrawal from Eastern Europe never occurred. Was this a result of intervention by the international financial institutions or a reflection of the banks' self-interest?

In spite of the tremendous economic shocks and prior imbalances, only three countries—Hungary, Latvia, and Romania—required IMF standby programs. Also, the European Commission, the World Bank, and Latvia's neighbors contributed substantially. The IMF acted even faster than usual, providing much more funding, also to finance their budget deficits, and it focused on a more limited set of key conditions than before. The other main international actor was the European Commission, which contributed more than the IMF to the Latvian program. Before the crisis, it

---

5. Lars Oxelheim, *International Financial Integration* (Heidelberg: Springer Verlag Berlin, 1990).

6. Anders Åslund, "Why Latvia Should Not Devalue," Realtime Economic Issues Watch, Peterson Institute for International Economics, December 9, 2008, www.piie.com.

was not clear how the European Commission and the IMF would interact, but the European Union accepted the IMF lead, offering substantial cofinancing and controlling the IMF programs. The cooperation between the IMF and the European Commission has worked surprisingly well, while the United States and the World Bank took a back seat. The EBRD and the European Investment Bank (EIB) focused on bank restructuring, while the ECB played no apparent role.[7]

The political economy of this adjustment has been quite remarkable. All crisis countries in this region undertook heroic fiscal adjustment programs. They cut public expenditures, public wages, and social transfers, while launching difficult structural reforms in health care and education. Many Western observers claimed that such big expenditure adjustments would be politically and socially impossible. They worried about regime change and collapse of democracy, but democracy persevered, and in fact social unrest and even populism have been minimal. Eight of the CEE-10 have changed government during the crisis, and the main crisis countries—Latvia, Hungary, and Romania—have changed government twice. Remarkably, in every case the new government was more radical in its adjustment policy than its predecessor, with the exception of the new Hungarian government. The center-right has benefited politically. At present, center-right parties rule nine of the CEE-10. Swift and radical problem resolution was evidently the preferred and most successful political approach, and it is the democratic center-right that has been doing so most convincingly.

The origins of the East European financial crisis were not surprising, but its resolution has been all the more so. The crisis countries have undertaken much more radical spending cuts than most economists considered possible. The fixed exchange rates of the currency board countries have not impeded adjustment but facilitated radical adjustment. The political economy of these countries has proven much more fortuitous than generally expected. Is this a peculiarity of these nations, or have their governments found a better solution than other governments? While globalization undoubtedly contributed to the crisis, it has also facilitated speedy crisis resolution.

The financial crisis has increased budget deficits and public debt in all the CEE-10 countries, but they have weathered the crisis better than most of the old members of the eurozone. Of the ten, nine remain below the Maastricht criterion of maximum public debt of 60 percent of GDP, while seven of the eleven original members of the eurozone currently exceed this threshold. By proving that their finances and economic systems are

---

7. Poland was approved for a flexible credit line from the IMF, since the ECB was not ready to offer Poland a swap credit, but this was a precautionary measure to safeguard sufficient liquidity, not a crisis measure.

comparatively stronger, the CEE-10 countries are giving new impetus to European convergence, even if the crisis has set their output back by a few years. Having gone through the steel bath of this crisis, these 10 eastern EU members will undoubtedly prove more competitive than the old EU members. Ironically, because the European Union treated the East European countries as second-class members, they faced hard budget constraints and pursued much more responsible fiscal policies than the first-class members of the eurozone. Therefore, they are catching up or overtaking the old EU members first in qualitative terms and later in economic welfare. The last shall be the first.

After this financial crisis resolution in the east, it is all the more striking how inadequate the crisis management was within the eurozone when Greece and other eurozone countries entered a severe financial crisis. Since the new EU members are doing qualitatively better than the old ones, this financial crisis is likely to reinforce convergence rather than divergence. The new EU members with currency boards remain determined to adopt the euro as early as they reasonably can, while the financial crisis in the eurozone has aroused new doubts in the countries with floating exchange rates.[8]

Maastricht Criteria and Euro Adoption

The euro was introduced in nonphysical form on January 1, 1999, while the bank notes were launched in January 2002. The original 11 members of the eurozone are Austria, Belgium, Finland, France, Germany, Ireland, Italy, Luxembourg, the Netherlands, Portugal, and Spain. Greece was admitted in 2001, taking the membership to 12. Slovenia entered in January 2007, Cyprus and Malta in 2008, and Slovakia in January 2009. At the beginning of 2009, out of the 27 EU members 16 belonged to the Economic and Monetary Union (EMU) and used the euro as their common currency. Among the new eastern EU members, the CEE-10, only three, Slovenia, Slovakia, and Estonia, have been admitted to the EMU so far. The other seven are obliged to enter the EMU, but no deadline exists. They have to fulfill five economic convergence criteria and receive political approval by the European Union.

An EU country that wants to adopt the euro must belong to the European Exchange Rate Mechanism (ERM II) for two years and fulfill the Maastricht criteria. These criteria are named after the Dutch town where the Treaty of the European Union was signed on February 7, 1992 by the then 12 members of the then European Community. These criteria remain in the current Lisbon Treaty or the Treaty on the Functioning of the Euro-

---

8. Increased doubts have been registered in opinion polls in the Czech Republic and Poland, as well as in Sweden and Denmark.

pean Union (TFEU). They are outlined in Article 140 in the TFEU and specified elsewhere:

- Price stability: Average inflation rate one year prior to entry must not exceed the average of the lowest three inflation rates of the EU member countries by more than 1.5 percentage points.
- The public sector deficit should not exceed 3 percent of GDP.
- The public debt should not surpass 60 percent of GDP.
- The normal fluctuation margins (+/−2.25 percent) within ERM II should be observed for at least two years.
- The average long-term nominal interest rate must not be higher than the average of the corresponding rates of the three lowest-inflation countries by more than 2 percentage points.[9]

A country's compliance with the Maastricht criteria is assessed by the European Commission in occasional economic convergence reports, which are decisive for a country's approval for euro adoption. The ECB also participates in this evaluation. However, the actual approval is a political decision, which is taken in several rounds by the council of eurozone finance ministers and all the EU finance ministers (the ECOFIN Council).

An important decision for each EU member outside of the eurozone was when to enter the ERM II. The ERM II rules prescribe a currency band of +/−15 percent around a "stable but adjustable central rate to the euro" or a preannounced, fixed exchange rate to the euro, but new entrants, the ECB, and the European Union (the ERM II committee) can negotiate the exact exchange rate regime. In reality, however, the band is much more narrow and effectively a peg with a narrow band.[10] Estonia and Lithuania entered the ERM II in 2004 and Latvia in 2005. Bulgaria has wanted ERM II membership but has so far not been admitted. The Czech Republic, Hungary, Poland, and Romania have not tried to enter the ERM II as yet.

The three countries, the United Kingdom, Denmark, and Sweden, that joined the European Union before the euro was introduced in 1999 had negotiated an exception and are not obliged to adopt the euro ever. Denmark pegged its exchange rate to the deutsche mark in 1982 and entered the ERM II in 1999. The new members admitted in 2004 and 2007 were not given the option to abstain from the euro.

All EU members, whether members of the EMU or not, are supposed

---

9. Article 140, Treaty on the Functioning of the European Union, *Official Journal of the European Union,* Information and Notices C 115, volume 51, May 9, 2008, available at http://eur-lex.europa.eu; Michael Marrese, *The Convergence of CEEMEA Countries as the Global Recession Ends* (New York: JP Morgan, July 29, 2009).

10. Marrese, *The Convergence of CEEMEA Countries;* European Union, "Acceding Countries and ERM-II," EFC/ECFIN/109/03 (Athens, April 5, 2003).

to comply with the fiscal Maastricht criteria, also called the Stability and Growth Pact (SGP), an EU agreement concluded in 1997 to bring fiscal discipline to the future EMU. If a eurozone country does not comply with the Maastricht criteria, the ECOFIN Council can initiate excessive deficit procedures, which can lead to severe penalties. However, because important euro countries violated these rules, excessive deficit procedures were never applied before the crisis.

Parallels to the East Asian Financial Crisis of 1997–98

The most obvious parallel to the East European crisis is the East Asian financial crisis in 1997–98, which hit Thailand, South Korea, Taiwan, Hong Kong, Indonesia, and Malaysia. The new EU members were reminiscent of these East Asian countries, especially South Korea. For years, the world had talked about the East Asian tigers and the East Asian economic miracle. Their open market economies and export orientation with high saving and investment rates had delivered persistent and high growth. Large capital inflows had resulted in excessive investment in real estate in a typical boom and bust cycle.

Finally, in 1997, the bubble burst. The East Asian tigers faced a "sudden stop" as capital inflows seized and were reversed.[11] At the time, that crisis was considered the end of their fortune. Joseph Stiglitz complained about "an unwarrantedly rapid pace toward financial and capital market liberalization" and that some "of the worst aspects of corruption, the so-called crony capitalism, will have to be checked."[12] Paul Krugman claimed that the East Asian growth miracle was caused by too much hard work and too large savings,[13] while others saw nothing but a standard financial crisis based on excessive success resulting in overheating.[14]

Raghuram Rajan has passed a tenable judgment: "The East Asian crisis was...largely a result of corporate overinvestment, in commercial real estate as well as manufacturing."[15] Unlike many previous emerging-market crises, the East Asian crisis did not involve large public deficits

---

11. This notion was coined by Rudiger Dornbusch, Ilan Goldfajn, and Rodrigo O. Valdés, "Currency Crises and Collapses," *Brookings Papers on Economic Activity* 26, 2: 219–93; Guillermo A. Calvo, "Capital Flows and Capital-Market Crises: The Simple Economics of Sudden Stops," *Journal of Applied Economics* 1, no. 1 (1998): 35–54.

12. Joseph E. Stiglitz, *Globalization and Its Discontents* (New York: Norton, 2002), 104, 127.

13. Paul Krugman, "The Myth of Asia's Miracle," *Foreign Affairs* 73, no. 6 (November–December 1994): 62.

14. Charles P. Kindleberger and Robert Aliber, *Manias, Panics, and Crashes*, 5th ed. (Hoboken, NJ: Wiley, 2005), 140–41, 156–58.

15. Raghuram Rajan, *Fault Lines: How Hidden Fractures Still Threaten the World Economy* (Princeton: Princeton University Press, 2010), 77.

or debts but entirely overheating in the private sector. This was the key parallel to the East European crisis of 2008. Rajan has lucidly explained how the East Asian financial crisis evolved from the perspective of foreign investors:

> Foreign investors who do not understand the murky insider relationships do three things. They minimize risks by offering only short-term loans so that they can pull their money out on short notice. They denominate payments in foreign currency so that their claims cannot be reduced by domestic inflation or a currency devaluation. And they lend through the local banks so that if they pull their money and the banks cannot repay it, the government will be drawn into supporting its banks to avoid widespread economic damage. Thus, foreign investors get an implicit government guarantee. The threat of inflicting collateral damage is what makes arm's-length foreign investors willing to entrust their money to the opaque relationship system.[16]

This picture of the East Asian crisis accurately portrays the East European situation with the main difference being that the West European banks owned most of the local banking system in Eastern Europe and were wedded to stay in these countries. But the three key characteristics—excessive short-term credits, loans in foreign currency, and lending through local banks—held true.

However, after only one year the East Asian financial crisis was over and these countries maintained their virtuous economic policies, which once again delivered stellar growth. As Simon Johnson and James Kwak write: "Even while outside observers are still despairing over corporate governance, macroeconomic management, and crony capitalism, growth picks up again. In 1999, the Korean economy grew by 11.1 percent."[17] Only one country, Indonesia, underwent regime change, with a successful transition to democracy and a more open market economy. Rather than a tragedy, the East Asian crisis was a brief upset that augured even greater success. The Russian financial crisis of 1998 and the Argentine crisis of 2001, by contrast, were profound fiscal crises, but even so the Russian crash initiated ten years of average annual economic growth of 7 percent.

In 2008, there was a broad appreciation of the similarities between the East Asian and East European crises. By and large, this understanding facilitated crisis resolution. Most experts and policymakers understood that this was a financial crisis and not a profound systemic crisis, which limited the demands for structural change. The crisis was seen as a temporary liquidity shortage and not as a solidity crisis, which persuaded international government creditors to provide large loans. Since the East Asians had returned their large loans in full and on time, the international community was prepared to finance substantial budget deficits too.

❋

16. Ibid., 12.

17. Simon Johnson and James Kwak, *13 Bankers: The Wall Street Takeover and the Next Financial Meltdown* (New York: Pantheon, 2010), 51.

A more controversial conclusion from the East Asian drama was that the best way out of a current account crisis to kickstart growth is devaluation. Since none of the East European countries with pegged exchange rates devalued, the exchange rate question is a key issue in the East European crisis resolution.

Structure of the Book

Chapters 2 and 3 provide a narrative of the East European crisis, its causes and eruption as well as resolution. The four ensuing chapters contain analysis of the most important aspects of the crisis. Chapter 4 discusses the prime economic question of the crisis: the exchange rate dilemma. Chapter 5 focuses on the expected banking crisis in Eastern Europe that did not really materialize. Chapter 6 examines the role of international actors, essentially the International Monetary Fund, the European Commission, the European Central Bank, and the United States. Chapter 7 considers why the CEE-10 countries acted so responsibly to resolve the crisis. Chapter 8 deals with implications of the eurozone fiscal crisis for Eastern Europe, and chapter 9 summarizes conclusions from the crisis for Eastern Europe.

In my analysis I focus on countries and institutions as the actors rather than on individuals. In order not to get lost in details, I minimize mentioning politicians and their differences and concentrate on the most controversial issues of principle. The one drawback I faced while writing this book early is that all statistics for 2010 are only forecasts. My primary sources of statistics cited throughout the book are the Eurostat database and the IMF's *World Economic Outlook*, which by and large overlap. Other sources are EBRD and JPMorgan statistics. The IMF website (www.imf.org) contains all official information about IMF agreements and programs.

2

Causes and Eruption of the Financial Crisis

...whoever has, to him more shall be given; and whoever does not have, even what he thinks he has shall be taken away from him.

—Luke 8:18

Central and Eastern Europe successfully transitioned to capitalism, deregulating prices and trade, stabilizing prices, and privatizing state property faster than anybody imagined.[1] From 1999 until 2008, these countries enjoyed high economic growth and stability. Never had this region experienced such a period of peace, freedom, national sovereignty, democracy, and rising economic welfare.

In 1989, the popular sentiment in these countries was "We want a normal society!" which meant democracy and a market economy based on private property and the rule of law. With the exception of Hungary, all these countries suffered from very high inflation during their postcommunist transition. In the early 1990s, Central Europe took the lead with radical market economic reform. Healthy competition prevailed between Poland, Hungary, and Czechoslovakia. From 1992, the Baltic countries caught up and went further in radical market reform. Bulgaria and Romania were lagging behind and experienced a serious financial crisis in 1996–97, which led to brief hyperinflation in Bulgaria. By 2008, all these countries were full-fledged market economies with close to 80 percent of their production originating in the private sector.

Another early popular slogan was "Return to Europe!" The European Union gave them all membership perspectives with generous free trade agreements. In 2004, eight East European countries were admitted to the

---

1. I have discussed this in my two books: *Building Capitalism: The Transformation of the Former Soviet Bloc* (New York: Cambridge University Press, 2002) and *How Capitalism Was Built: The Transformation of Central and Eastern Europe, Russia, and Central Asia* (New York: Cambridge University Press, 2007).

European Union, and in 2007 Bulgaria and Romania were let in. These 10 countries—the CEE-10 as I call them (box 1.1)—are the focus of this study. EU accession started a massive credit and investment boom in the new EU members, as many companies in the old EU members outsourced their production to the new EU members. Their goods and capital markets were completely open, and many of their citizens emigrated to EU countries to earn much higher salaries. In parallel, all these countries became members of the North Atlantic Treaty Organization (NATO), which reinforced their sense of security and belonging to the West.

The years 2000–08 represented a period of unprecedented economic growth. The CEE-10 fall into three subregions: The turbo region of the three Baltic countries (Estonia, Latvia, and Lithuania) had an average unweighted annual growth of 7 percent, peaking at 10 percent in 2006. Central Europe (the Czech Republic, Hungary, Poland, Slovakia, and Slovenia) had a more moderate average growth of 4.4 percent, and Southeastern Europe (Bulgaria and Romania) fared somewhat better at 5.7 percent a year (figure 2.1).[2]

Therefore, the financial crisis was all the more shocking, but the outcomes differed greatly. In late 2007, the Estonian and Latvian economies started cooling, and in 2008, Latvia's GDP declined by 4.6 percent and Estonia's by 3.6 percent. In 2009, all but Poland experienced large economic slumps; Poland enjoyed a modest growth of 1.7 percent. The Czech Republic, Slovakia, Hungary, and Bulgaria faced decreases of around 5 percent of GDP in line with the average eurozone contraction of 4.1 percent. Romania experienced a decline of 7.2 percent, Slovenia 7.8 percent, and the Baltic states 14 to 18 percent (figure 2.2). In 2009, no other economies in the world faced such contractions as the Baltic states apart from Ukraine and Armenia.[3] What were the causes of these large contractions and their variations?

Causes of the Crisis

The East European financial crisis fits perfectly with Charles Kindleberger's dictum:

> The standard model of the sequence of events that leads to financial crises is that a shock leads to an economic expansion that then morphs into an economic boom; euphoria develops and then there is a pause in the increase in asset prices. Distress is likely to follow as asset prices begin to decline. The pattern is biological in its regularity. A panic is likely and then a crash may follow.[4]

---

2. Throughout this book I use unweighted averages, as the purpose is to compare the effects of economic policy.

3. International Monetary Fund, *World Economic Outlook* (Washington, April 2010).

4. Charles P. Kindleberger and Robert Aliber, *Manias, Panics, and Crashes*, 5th ed. (Hoboken, NJ: Wiley, 2005), 90.

Figure 2.1   Real GDP growth, 2000–10e

percent annual growth

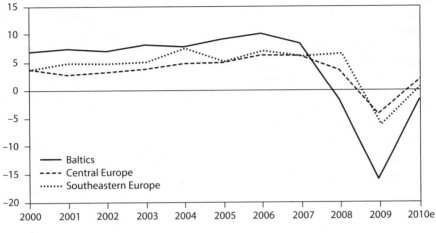

e = estimate

Sources: European Bank for Reconstruction and Development, www.ebrd.com; IMF, *World Economic Outlook*, October 2009; JP Morgan statistics; Eurostat database, http://epp.eurostat.ec. europa.eu.

Figure 2.2   Real GDP decline, 2009

percent annual change

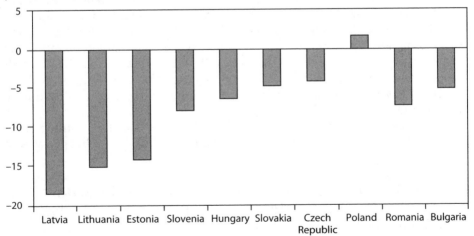

Sources: JP Morgan statistics; CISstat, www.cisstat.com; Eurostat database, http://epp.eurostat.ec. europa.eu (accessed on March 28, 2010).

The Lehman Brothers bankruptcy and its ensuing credit crunch unleashed financial panic in Eastern Europe, but it was only the catalyst. Financial problems in the CEE-10 were profound and ubiquitous. Multiple preconditions of crisis were evident: excessive current account deficits, large foreign debt, small currency reserves, substantial currency mismatches, huge credit expansion, sharp real estate price rises, and rising inflation.[5] By almost all indicators, overheating was worst in the countries with fixed exchange rates: Bulgaria, Estonia, Latvia, and Lithuania.

In the early postcommunist transformation, East European economic growth was driven by export demand,[6] but gradually all these countries ratcheted up current account deficits, and their growth became increasingly driven by consumption and investment in real estate. The old rule of thumb is that a current account deficit of more than 4 to 5 percent of GDP is dangerous. In 2002, Estonia's current account deficit soared to double digits as a share of GDP, and in 2007 five of the CEE-10 countries had large deficits: Bulgaria, Estonia, Latvia, Lithuania, and Romania (figure 2.3).

A large current account deficit is not necessarily dangerous if it is financed with foreign direct investment (FDI), as capital may move in permanently.[7] Impressively, FDI more or less balanced the current account deficit in Slovakia, the Czech Republic, Bulgaria, Poland, and Slovenia. The other five CEE-10 countries—Latvia, Estonia, Lithuania, Hungary, and Romania—whose current account deficits were not fully financed by FDI were most badly hit by the crisis. Current account deficits not financed by FDI appear to be the single best predictor of crisis in countries.[8]

The current account deficits in the CEE-10 accumulated into rising foreign debt. By 2008, five countries in the region had total foreign debt (both public and private) exceeding their GDP: Bulgaria, Estonia, Hungary, Latvia, and Slovenia (figure 2.4). Even so Slovenia largely escaped the crisis, apparently saved by its early adoption of the euro in 2007, which averted any international liquidity squeeze. Nor did Bulgaria with its uniquely large FDI suffer much. Surprisingly, the foreign debt said little about the risk of crisis.

The real effective exchange rate (REER) is usually a strong indicator of overheating leading to overvaluation. But the exchange rates of

5. Morris Goldstein, "Emerging-Market Financial Crises: Lessons and Prospects" (speech, 2007 Annual Meeting, Institute of International Finance, Washington, October 20, 2007).

6. Åslund, *How Capitalism Was Built*, 79–80.

7. Marek Dabrowski, "Rethinking Balance of Payments Constraints in a Globalized World" in *Challenges of Globalization: Imbalances and Growth*, eds. Anders Åslund and Marek Dabrowski (Washington: Peterson Institute for International Economics, 2008).

8. Zsolt Darvas and Jean Pisani-Ferry, "Avoiding a New European Divide," Bruegel Policy Brief no. 10 (Brussels: Bruegel, December 2008).

Figure 2.3   Current account deficit as share of GDP, 2006 and 2007

percent of GDP

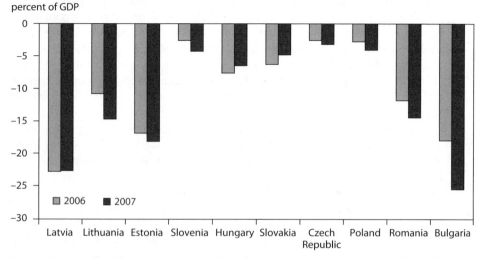

Sources: European Bank for Reconstruction and Development, www.ebrd.com; IMF, *World Economic Outlook*, October 2009 (accessed on March 30, 2010).

Figure 2.4   Gross foreign debt as share of GDP, end 2008

percent of GDP

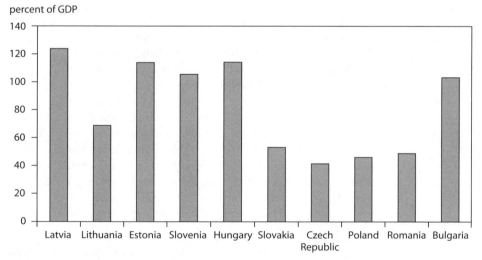

Source: European Bank for Reconstruction and Development, www.ebrd.com (accessed on October 28, 2009 and January 28, 2010).

all the postcommunist countries were deeply depressed around 1990, warranting a large initial recovery. Moreover, their high productivity also justified a sharp rise in REERs, but the statistical picture is confusing (figure 2.5). Romania stands out: Its REER rose by no less than 80 percent in the course of a decade. From 2003 to 2008, Slovakia, the Czech Republic, and Poland—three countries with inflation targeting—saw their nominal effective exchange rates rise by 30 to 40 percent, which impeded capital inflows and inflation. The other countries saw minimal nominal exchange rate changes.[9]

International currency reserves attracted little attention, but they were small (figure 2.6). Susan Schadler of the International Monetary Fund (IMF) noticed: "…these countries stand out among emerging markets for having relatively small official reserves compared to their short-term external debt."[10] Three months of imports are usually considered the minimum permissible level of reserves, but by the end of 2008, only Latvia, Poland, Romania, and Bulgaria just about exceeded this level. In addition, reserves were needed to balance sudden capital outflows. The small reserves corresponded to chosen policy. The countries with floating exchange rates were prepared for large exchange rate adjustments, while the currency board countries had a fixed regime of reserves covering their money supply. The two Economic and Monetary Union (EMU) countries, Slovakia and Slovenia, depended on the European Central Bank (ECB). All the CEE-10 countries relied on the European Union, which rendered them vulnerable.

The most indebted countries also suffered from currency mismatches, another crisis predictor. Foreign currency, primarily euro but sometimes Swiss francs, was used extensively for domestic loans, both corporate loans and household mortgages, because interest rates were significantly lower for foreign currency loans and borrowers did not expect any depreciation. The three Baltic countries, Hungary, and Romania had more than half of domestic loans in foreign currency (figure 2.7). The Czech Republic stood out because for a long time Czech domestic interest rates were actually lower than euro rates.[11] In Poland and Slovakia domestic credits in foreign currencies were restricted by a combination of stricter bank regulation and floating exchange rates, which made people aware of currency risks.

The large capital inflows boosted domestic money supply. Both the Baltics and Southeastern Europe saw rapid monetary expansion. In

9. Bas B. Bakker and Anne-Marie Gulde, "The Credit Boom in the EU New Member States: Bad Luck or Bad Policies?" IMF Working Paper 10/130 (Washington: International Monetary Fund, 2010), 35.

10. Susan Schadler, "Are Large External Imbalances in Central Europe Sustainable," in *Challenges of Globalization: Imbalances and Growth*, eds. Anders Åslund and Marek Dabrowski (Washington: Peterson Institute for International Economics, 2008), 38.

11. I owe this observation to Bálazs Égert.

Figure 2.5 Real effective exchange rate growth, 1999–2008

index, EU-27 = 100

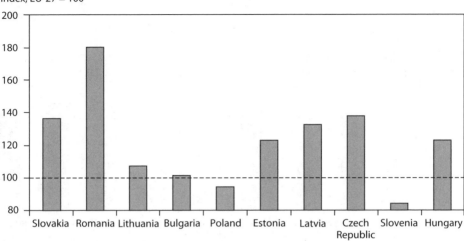

Source: Eurostat database, http://epp.eurostat.ec.europa.eu (accessed on May 27, 2010); author's calculations.

Figure 2.6 International currency reserves as share of imports, end 2008

months of imports

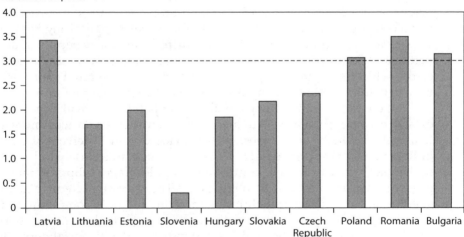

Sources: IMF Data Template on International Reserves and Foreign Currency Liquidity, www.imf.org; United Nations Economic Commission for Europe, www.unece.org (accessed on April 13, 2010); author's calculations.

Figure 2.7   Share of foreign currency loans in total domestic credit, 2007

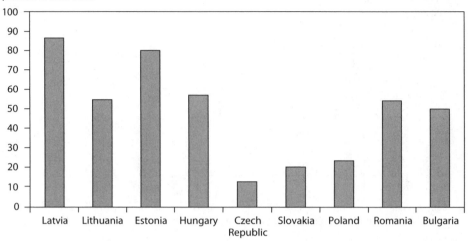

percent of total loans

Source: Zolt Darvas and Jean Pisani-Ferry, *Avoiding a New European Divide*, Bruegel Policy Brief No. 10: 2 (Brussels: Bruegel, December 2008), www.bruegel.org.

the Baltics it peaked at 39 percent in 2005, but then it decelerated fast, growing by only 4 percent in 2008, when output contraction started. Similarly, Romania and Bulgaria experienced a monetary expansion of 30 to 35 percent a year from 2004 to 2007. Central Europe by contrast persistently had a constrained monetary policy, with the money supply rising by 9 to 12 percent a year (figure 2.8). Behind the increase in money supply in the Baltics and Southeastern Europe lay even more radical increases in bank credit, which is the main explanation of both the more rapid monetary growth before 2008 and the more severe crisis than in Central Europe.

Yet, the total credit volume remained comparatively small as a share of GDP because it had been extremely depressed after the postcommunist financial crisis in the early 1990s. In 2008 it varied from 39 percent of GDP in Romania to 95 percent of GDP in Estonia, which was closely followed by Latvia.[12] None of these countries had high leverage, subprime mortgages, or collateralized debt obligations. The excessive credit expansion boosted economic growth in the medium and even long term, but eventually it caused a bust. This observation casts doubt on the extensive literature of regression analysis that indicates that financial depth is beneficial to economic growth. A credit boom can build up for a long time but eventually it will end, and a period of deleveraging is likely to follow and reduce growth.

---

12. Bakker and Gulde, "The Credit Boom in the EU New Member States," 15.

Figure 2.8 Monetary expansion, 2004–08

M2 percent annual change

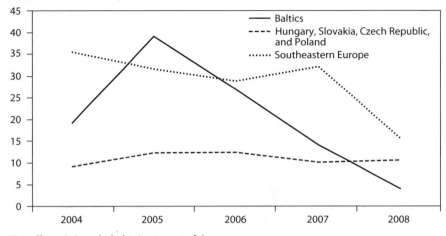

Note: Slovenia is excluded as it was part of the eurozone.

Source: IMF, *International Financial Statistics,* www.imf.org (accessed on May 5 and May 10, 2010); author's calculations.

Not surprisingly, housing prices were closely related to credit expansion. They rose massively in the four currency board countries from 2003 to 2007, most of all in Latvia, where they skyrocketed by 240 percent. Estonia came next with a tripling of housing prices, while they rose by some 150 percent in Bulgaria and Lithuania.[13]

After disinflation in the early 2000s, inflation started rising again after 2005 because of the credit boom. In 2007 only two countries had less than 3 percent annual inflation (Poland and Slovakia), while Latvia had double-digit inflation (figure 2.9). In 2008, all the three Baltic countries and Bulgaria—the four countries with fixed exchange rates—recorded double-digit inflation, pricing themselves out of the market, which resulted in large current account deficits. The expansion of the money supply did not result in an equal amount of inflation because the demand for money and monetization grew sharply, as the velocity of money was declining.

The fiscal performance of the new EU members varied greatly. Central European countries had large budget deficits in the early 2000s but one after the other moved within the Maastricht budget ceiling of 3 percent of GDP: Slovenia in 2002, Slovakia in 2003, the Czech Republic in 2006, and Poland in 2007. Only Hungary never did. Its budget deficit culminated at 9.3 percent of GDP in the global boom year of 2006.

The currency board countries, by contrast, were fiscally virtuous.

---

13. Ibid., 19.

Figure 2.9 Inflation, 2007 and 2008

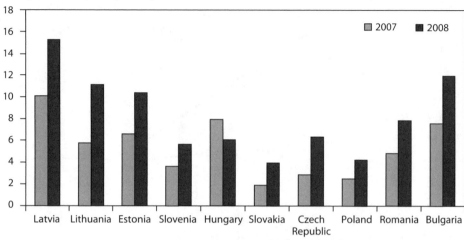

average consumer prices (percent)

Source: IMF, *World Economic Outlook*, April 2010, www.imf.org (accessed on May 4, 2010).

Bulgaria and Estonia had persistent and significant budget surpluses, while Latvia and Lithuania almost balanced their budgets. Romania complied with the budget ceiling from 2002 to 2007 (figure 2.10). Yet this was a time of extraordinary boom, and a budget policy aiming at balance over the business cycle would have called for substantial budget surpluses in all these countries.

The budget deficits said little about a country's vulnerability to financial crisis because all, except Hungary, had small or moderate public debts. With public debt at 73 percent of GDP at the end of 2008, Hungary was the only East European country to exceed the Maastricht ceiling of 60 percent of GDP. For most countries, public debt as a share of GDP fell steadily until 2008, when the unweighted average was 26 percent (figure 2.11).

This crisis was not about postcommunist transition. The severity of the crisis depended almost entirely on financial factors. The clearest evidence is that Central Asia did not suffer much.[14] Nor was this a crisis of crony capitalism or corruption. All the East European countries ranked reasonably high on Transparency International's Corruption Perceptions Index. In 2009, Estonia and Slovenia topped the lot, sharing the 27th place out of 180 countries, while Bulgaria and Romania shared the 71st place, with the rest in the middle ranking from 46 to 56. This is no stellar perfor-

---

14. European Bank for Reconstruction and Development, *Transition Report 2009* (London, 2009).

Figure 2.10　Budget balance, 2000–10e

percent of GDP

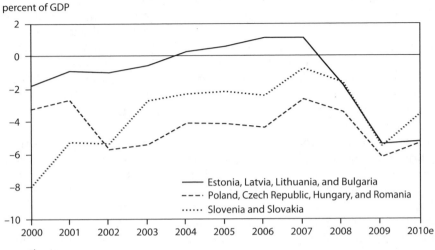

e = estimate

Sources: European Bank for Reconstruction and Development, *Transition Reports*, 2006, 2007, and 2008, www.ebrd.com (accessed on April 12, 2010); JP Morgan CEEMEA Economic Outlook Summary, March 26, 2010; CISstat database, www.cisstat.com (accessed on March 30, 2010); author's calculations.

Figure 2.11　Public debt as share of GDP, end 2008

percent of GDP

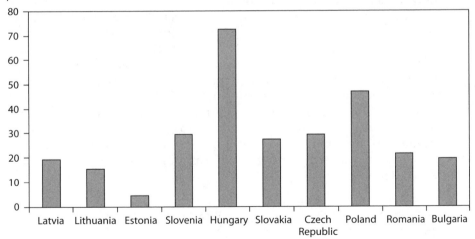

Source: European Bank for Reconstruction and Development, www.ebrd.com (accessed on April 13, 2010).

mance, but it is decent. All but Bulgaria and Romania were judged less corrupt than Italy (placed 63).[15]

Central Europe, the subregion most integrated with the European Union, largely escaped the financial crisis (apart from fiscally irresponsible Hungary). Thus, deep integration into the European economy appears to have been advantageous. The European Union, however, does not mark any dividing line, as the Baltic countries were the worst hit. Poland fared better than Slovakia and Slovenia, not to mention Germany or Southern Europe, although it did not belong to the EMU, so the eurozone was no salvation either.

The conclusion from this survey of precrisis indicators is that the main culprit was significant current account deficits not financed by FDI. This runs against Guillermo Calvo's earlier conclusion: "Large current account deficits are dangerous *independently of how they are financed*."[16] Presumably European integration went so much further that capital movements were much more permanent than in Calvo's largely Latin American emerging-market world. Another negative indicator was double-digit inflation caused by excessive credit expansion, and a third was a large share of domestic loans in foreign currency, while the state of public finances was relatively good.

Developments after the global financial crisis struck were not surprising. Even in a world of large global imbalances, Central and Eastern Europe had the largest current account deficits because of low saving rates and high domestic investment rates, while their reserves were small and foreign debts high.[17] As the initial crisis concerned the current account rather than the fiscal situation, exchange rate and monetary policy naturally mattered more than fiscal policy.

Hungary stood out because of its patently weak public finances since the 1980s, and it fell like ripe fruit in the global financial storm. Reviewing the statistics of end 2007, one would expect the three Baltic countries and Bulgaria to enter serious financial crises because of high inflation undermining their competitiveness, large current account deficits, large foreign debt, and small currency reserves. But the surprise is that only Latvia required IMF support. All the Baltic countries suffered big output drops, whereas their stamina was greater than most expected. Among the remaining five countries, Romania was somewhat weak in most regards, especially with its rapid real appreciation, while Poland, the Czech Republic, and Slovakia looked solid, and Slovenia decent.

---

15. Transparency International, Corruption Perceptions Index 2009, available at www.transparency.org (accessed on July 17, 2010).

16. Guillermo A. Calvo, "Capital Flows and Capital-Market Crises: The Simple Economics of Sudden Stops," *Journal of Applied Economics* 1, no. 1 (1998): 35–54 (emphasis in original).

17. Schadler, "Are Large External Imbalances in Central Europe Sustainable," 17.

Eruption of the Crisis

The global financial crisis was triggered by the decline of US housing prices, which peaked in the fall of 2006.[18] The subprime mortgage crisis erupted in August 2007, when two large Bear Stearns hedge funds collapsed and two German state financial institutions went under, as they had invested in collateralized debt obligations based on subprime mortgages. The global financial crisis had started.

Yet, seemingly isolated incidents continued to occur. In September 2007, a classical bank run started on Britain's Northern Rock, a mortgage provider not covered by the British partial deposit insurance scheme. When its finances were in doubt, its depositors panicked, forming long queues to withdraw their money.

In late 2007, the financial bubble started bursting in the two most overheated East European countries, Latvia and Estonia, as well as in Kazakhstan in Central Asia. They had all financed major real estate booms with foreign bank loans. In Latvia, housing prices had skyrocketed by 240 percent in 2003–07 and in Estonia by 200 percent.[19] The trigger was a combination of domestic bank inspections tightening credit rules and a few foreign banks getting cold feet over their risk exposure and belatedly starting to slow down their lending. As a consequence, house prices started declining, and with them investment and private consumption.

In March 2008, the fifth largest US investment bank Bear Stearns failed and it was quickly taken over by JP Morgan without impact on Eastern Europe. More important was that in April 2008 the giant Swiss bank UBS reported huge losses from American subprime mortgages. UBS played a central role in the carry trade of low-interest loans in Swiss francs to the wholesale credit market that financed banks in Eastern Europe.

In the spring of 2008, inflation peaked at double digits in the four CEE-10 countries with currency boards, reaching as high as 18 percent in Latvia. The high inflation priced the Baltic countries and Bulgaria out of the market. With smaller bank inflows, imports started declining, which reduced the current account deficits, most sharply so in Latvia from 23 percent of GDP in 2007 to a still high 13 percent in 2008. Gradually, one bank after the other tightened its lending.[20] Analyst Lars Christensen of Danske Bank claimed that a major financial crisis was under way. He was

---

18. Olivier Blanchard, "The Perfect Storm," *Finance & Development* (June 2010): 37.

19. Bakker and Gulde, "The Credit Boom in the EU New Member States," 19.

20. The three Swedish banks that dominated in the Baltics were Swedbank, SEB, and Nordea. SEB started constraining its credits in summer 2007, Swedbank followed in late 2007, while Nordea took the opportunity to gain market share in 2008.

accused of having provoked Latvians to exchange their lats for euros in the spring of 2007 in fear of imminent devaluation.[21]

Yet, until the Lehman Brothers bankruptcy in September 2008, the conventional wisdom was that the financial storms would pass continental Western Europe and most of Eastern Europe. Mitigating factors were that the East European countries had little financial depth or leverage. Mortgages and consumer loans were limited, and subprime loans and collateralized debt obligations were literally unknown. As late as July 2008, in Yalta, Ukraine, IMF Managing Director Dominique Strauss-Kahn spoke about the financial crisis as an American crisis, ignoring that Ukraine's inflation had just reached 31 percent in May 2008.

In July 2008, commodity prices peaked. The oil price hit $147 per barrel, and steel as well as nonferrous metals reached their highs too. Immediately afterward, all commodity prices started falling, but since the peak had been so high, this was initially seen as normalization rather than the beginning of a drastic fall. Yet, it hurt the large commodity exporters Russia, Kazakhstan, and Ukraine just to the east of the CEE-10.

The catalyst of the financial crisis in Eastern Europe was a so-called sudden stop.[22] After the Lehman Brothers bankruptcy on September 15, 2008, global liquidity froze, and the worst-exposed countries found themselves excluded from global finance, in particular faraway countries with large current account deficits and large foreign debt from overleveraged Western financial institutions. Several big West European banks failed within a month, and in early October Iceland's three big banks collapsed and were taken over by the government, leaving Iceland in profound financial crisis.

The carry trade in short-term Swiss franc credits disappeared. The ECB tried vigorously to replace them with euro credits at negligible interest rates to banks in the EMU. Other independent central banks in the European Union, such as the Swedish Riksbank and Denmark's National Bank, acted similarly, but liquidity was very scarce. Suddenly, closely related partners were crucial for access to credit. Particularly badly hit were banks financing themselves on the international wholesale market with short-term credit.

At a cocktail party at the annual meetings of the IMF and the World Bank on October 10, 2008, a triumphant top IMF official whispered to me: "We have three new clients!" I could deduce that they were Hungary, Ukraine, and Pakistan. The IMF was back in business. Soon, many more clients would turn up.

---

21. "Lars Christensen, you are being laughed at!" prygi.blogspot.com, January 5, 2008, available at http://prygi.blogspot.com/2008/01/lars-christensen-you-are-being-laughed.html (accessed on June 12, 2010).

22. Sebastian Edwards, "Capital Controls, Sudden Stops and Current Account Reversals," NBER Working Paper 11170 (Cambridge, MA: National Bureau of Economic Research, 2005).

Hungary was an accident waiting to happen, having been close to fiscally unsustainable during the boom years because of excessive budget deficits. With its large public debt, Hungary was dependent on regular sales of government bonds to foreign investors. In early October 2008, foreign investors stopped buying Hungarian bonds and sold more than $2 billion of Hungarian government securities because of the global credit crunch. As capital flight caught on, the freely floating Hungarian forint depreciated by 17 percent in relation to the euro in October 2008. On October 22, the Hungarian central bank reacted to the panic by shock-raising the policy rate from 8.5 to 11.5 percent a year.[23] On October 28, Hungary concluded an IMF standby agreement.

All local banks in the region that were dependent on short-term financing from the international wholesale market suffered badly. As the financing in short swaps in Swiss francs halted, access to ECB financing became vital. Hardest hit was Ukraine, where half a dozen domestically owned banks quickly collapsed in the wake of a big depreciation. Within the European Union, the local bank with the biggest domestic market share was Parex Bank in Latvia. Owned by two Latvian citizens, it was one of the few big survivors from the first wave of Soviet private banks. It had long wooed Russian clients with extraordinary chutzpah. In 1992, Parex advertised: "We exchange all currencies and ask no questions." In 2005, it announced that Riga was closer to Moscow than Switzerland and that all at Parex spoke Russian. In a last daring advertisement, its billboards in Stockholm offered 6.5 percent a year deposit rates in Swedish kronor. Parex collapsed at the outset of the crisis, which made the government fear the country would run out of international currency reserves and forced it to call in the IMF in October 2008. After long negotiations, an IMF standby agreement was concluded on December 19. Although Latvia was also an accident waiting to happen, it could have held out for several months without an IMF program, if it had not been for Parex Bank. It was mainly the resolution of Parex that complicated the IMF negotiations.

Exchange rates sharply diverged with the credit crunch. In this neighborhood, Sweden, Poland, the Czech Republic, Hungary, and Romania had floating exchange rates, and in late 2008 Russia and Ukraine let their currencies depreciate sharply. Two contradictory worries arose. The first was that devaluation would break certain nations' banking systems. In January and February 2009, Poland posed the primary concern, because its exchange rate fell most within the European Union. The domestic loans in hard currency were reasonably safe as they were reserved for the privileged upper middle class, but international financing of the banks became dangerously expensive.[24] In the spring of 2009, the most depreciated cur-

---

23. Paul Marer, "Global Crises and Eastern Europe," *Acta Oeconomica* 60, no. 1 (March 2010): 21, 30.

24. I owe this point to Jeffrey Anderson.

rencies started recovering. Fortunately, Poland and the other countries withstood this depreciation crisis for the banks and therefore this scare is often forgotten.

Countries with the euro, or with currencies pegged to the euro, faced the more publicized, somewhat exaggerated problem of an overvalued euro exchange rate. A review of exports in 2009 suggests that industrial structure was far more important than exchange rate. EMU member Slovakia saw the biggest decline of 16.5 percent, but it was also greatly dependent on car exports, as was its neighbor the Czech Republic, whose exports contracted similarly by 15.8 percent, although it has a floating exchange rate. By contrast, nearby oil exporter Russia with a greatly depreciated ruble faced a drop of 36 percent in its exports. Exports of Lithuania and Latvia contracted less, 15.5 and 13.9 percent, respectively.[25] Naturally, the high euro exchange rate in the midst of the crisis was bad for the eurozone and countries with euro pegs, but the damage was comparatively limited.

Also, Romania needed an IMF standby agreement, though less obviously so. It had problems with the maturity structure of its public debt, which required large, early rollover, although public debt was only 22 percent of GDP in 2008, when its budget deficit stopped at 4.9 percent of GDP. Its current account deficit of 12 percent of GDP, which was caused by its excessive real effective exchange rate, was worrisome, and little was financed with foreign direct investment. Yet its total foreign debt was just 49 percent of GDP. Under normal circumstances, Romania might have been all right. But its politics were messy. The Romanian government concluded an IMF standby agreement on March 25, 2009.

Rather surprisingly, Lithuania and Estonia did not require any IMF program or EU support and resolved their severe hardship on their own. In early June 2009, as the Latvian crisis intensified for the last time, they faced a final threat of devaluation. After Latvia had received renewed EU financing in July 2009, the crisis abated in the whole region.

In the winter of 2008–09, a new worry was that the international financial institutions would run out of funding, as the IMF had funds of only $250 billion available. The newly revitalized group of 20 largest economies in the world (G-20) came to the IMF's support. At its April 2, 2009, summit in London, the G-20 urged the world to boost IMF funding to $1.1 trillion. As a consequence, the IMF received far more funding than all other international financial institutions together. Arguably, this G-20 decision marked the end of the credit crunch. Also, the US stress test of the biggest banks published in May 2009 may be credited with easing the liquidity squeeze.

The Czech Republic, Poland, Slovakia, and Slovenia did not experience any particular financial crisis, with their banking systems almost

---

25. Bakker and Gulde, "The Credit Boom in the EU New Member States," 22.

entirely owned by European banks. They could allow their budget deficits to bulge and their monetary policy to ease. Poland was the best-performing economy in Europe. Like the Czech Republic, it could afford an actual fiscal stimulus and a loosening of its monetary policy as the credit crunch started, but it got a scare in early 2009, when its exchange rate dropped deep. Poland's concern was limited access to international liquidity, and nobody was prepared to give it swap credits. Therefore, it turned to the IMF, being the first customer of a precautionary flexible credit line facility of $20.5 billion in May 2009 after the crisis had abated.[26] This facility had been introduced in March 2009 and marked an important shift from ex post conditionality for crisis countries to ex ante conditionality for countries with sound fundamentals.[27] Another customer was Mexico.

With the eruption of the Greek financial crisis in the spring of 2010, the greatest worry for the East European banking system was collateral damage from the Greek financial crisis. Greek banks held 30 and 18 percent of Bulgarian and Romanian banking assets, respectively. Both countries responded with large new public spending cuts, which resulted in the largest organized protests since the outbreak of the financial crisis in the region.[28]

In early June 2010, a curious crisis arose in Hungary. A couple of representatives of the Young Democrat Party, which had just won parliamentary elections, warned that a Greek crisis with default was possible in Hungary. The apparent purpose of these statements was to relieve the new government of its rather populist election promises and facilitate further austerity, but nervous financial-market operators perceived this as an assessment of the true state of affairs and began selling all kinds of Hungarian assets.[29] Yet this crisis of confidence was revived in July, when the Hungarian government publicly rejected IMF demands for further budget cuts and the IMF broke off negotiations. Hungary remains an exception in the East European financial crisis.

In early 2010 public focus moved from the external indebtedness of Eastern Europe and risks to its banking system to the public indebtedness of the PIGS (Portugal, Italy, Greece, and Spain) and the possible risk of sovereign default, especially in Greece.

---

26. IMF, "IMF Executive Board Approves $20.58 Arrangement for Poland under the flexible credit line," press release no. 09/153, May 6, 2009.

27. Olivier Jeanne, Jonathan Ostry, and Jeromin Zettelmeyer, "A Theory of International Crisis Lending and IMF Conditionality," IMF Working Paper 08/236 (Washington: International Monetary Fund, 2008).

28. Miroslav Plojhar and Yarkin Cebeci, "Romania and Bulgaria Announced Large Public Spending Cuts" (JP Morgan Emerging Europe Economic Research, May 7, 2010).

29. Neil Buckley, "Hungary Gives Second Warning about 'Grave' Risk of Default," *Financial Times*, June 5–6, 2010.

3

Political Economy of Crisis Resolution

Coming together is a beginning; keeping together is progress;
working together is success.

—Henry Ford

The East European financial crisis was quickly and decisively resolved. The International Monetary Fund (IMF) stabilization programs for the three main crisis countries in the CEE-10—Hungary, Latvia, and Romania—were supported with more financing than ever before because of substantial European cofinancing. The other countries in the region facing hardship, notably Estonia and Lithuania, adopted domestic anticrisis programs, while the rest did not face equally severe crises. Early and radical fiscal adjustment was the common feature in all these programs, and the results were swift and positive. The governments did what they had promised, and economic recoveries have been reassuring. All these countries are forecast to return to economic growth in the second half of 2010 (figure 2.1).

But it did not look this good in the winter of 2008–09. All three main crisis countries changed governments twice during the crisis and observers worried about political instability, but each new government was more effective than its predecessor in pursuing anticrisis policies until a new government of young democrats entered the stage in Hungary. In 2008, Hungary saw many street protests and the rise of a vocal far-right party, Jobbik. Latvia was shocked by its January 13, 2009, riots, and Lithuania faced similar riots the next day. Until the fall of 2009, international opinion was that Latvia and perhaps the other currency board countries, Estonia, Lithuania, and Bulgaria, would have to devalue. To the surprise of many, none of the four devalued, and only Latvia needed an IMF program, which caused serious tension between the IMF and the European Union.

It is remarkable how the four currency board countries managed their crises in spite of intimidating foreign imbalances and large output falls. The rigid currency board system facilitated responsible fiscal policy and minimized public debt, but it also caused overheating. The popularity of the currency boards made it politically easier to resolve the crisis. They left minimal room for financial instruments, making it very difficult to speculate against these currencies.

Political developments were rather counterintuitive. Most of these countries had unstable governments and highly fragmented parliaments with five to seven parties represented, but the fragmentation caused little harm and political instability was largely positive, facilitating swift improvement of executives. The only country where governments sat their full mandate periods until 2009 and a government was reelected was Hungary, which pursued the worst fiscal policy. Of the crisis countries, most changed governments during the crisis, and all the new governments were more radical reform governments than their predecessors. Only the most radical free marketers, the Estonian government, survived the crisis.

In virtually every CEE-10 country, the eventual prime minister, minister of finance, or chairman of the central bank were strong leaders and heroes of financial stabilization, while weaklings were left by the political wayside. Strikingly, nobody called for regime change in these democracies. Nor did any eastern EU country display any left-wing tendencies. The communists were obliterated, while socialists were marginalized, as the moderate center-right made headway in elections in Lithuania, Romania, Bulgaria, Hungary, the Czech Republic, and Slovakia in 2008–10. Populism was present but rather mild.

The dominant political theme before the crisis was corruption. Bulgarian political scientist Ivan Krastev has pointed out that corruption always weighs against the incumbent government, so when corruption dominates an election campaign, the sitting government is likely to lose.[1] By and large, the politicians who have pursued austerity policies have also acted against corruption, as both policies combat unjustified privileges. Romanian President Traian Băsescu, Bulgarian Prime Minister Boyko Borisov, and Latvian Prime Minister Valdis Dombrovskis made their careers as anticorruption fighters, while the Romanian, Bulgarian, Hungarian, and Lithuanian socialists lost elections because they were tainted by corruption.

The IMF took the lead in the stabilization programs, while the European Commission sat in on the IMF negotiations with the crisis governments and provided funding from its balance-of-payments facility for EU countries outside the Economic and Monetary Union (EMU). The IMF concluded its standby agreements first, and the European Commission guaranteed financing at the same time in separate but similar agreements

---

1. Ivan Krastev, *Shifting Obsessions: Three Essays on Politics of Anti-Corruption* (Budapest: CEU Press, 2004).

with the crisis countries that were formally concluded slightly later. The World Bank, the European Bank for Reconstruction and Development (EBRD), and the European Investment Bank (EIB) played subsidiary roles, focusing on bank restructuring.

Hungary: Straightforward Crisis Resolution

Hungary had enjoyed seven years of decent economic growth of slightly more than 4 percent a year from 2000 to 2006, but its public finances were in tatters. During the five good years 2002–06, Hungary had an average budget deficit of 7.9 percent of GDP because of outsized social transfers. It was the only East European country with truly populist politics, as its two dominant parties, the ruling socialists and the opposition Alliance of Young Democrats (FIDESZ), competed in proposing the most generous social benefits. The incumbent socialist party won the parliamentary elections in April 2006. That year, the Hungarian budget deficit peaked at 9.3 percent of GDP. Something had to be done. Socialist Prime Minister Ferenc Gyurcsány—who had started out as a young communist leader and then gone on to make a fortune in the private sector—tried to tighten the purse strings, but that was not easy since it contradicted his campaign promises.

An audio recording from a closed-door meeting of the socialist party in May 2006 emerged in September 2006. At that meeting, Gyurcsány admitted, "We have obviously been lying for the last one and a half to two years." With these words he denounced his party's prior populism, but his confessing to systematic lying provoked public outrage, with thousands of demonstrators taking to the streets every day for several weeks. Gyurcsány refused to resign, but his political authority was mortally wounded. He tightened the budget somewhat, but alone among the new EU members, Hungary fulfilled only one of the five Maastricht criteria in 2007, when economic growth dwindled to 1.1 percent, while all the other East European countries were booming.[2]

The September 2008 credit crunch hit Hungary instantly. In early October, the government asked for an IMF program. On October 28, 2008, the government concluded a 17-month standby agreement with the IMF with financing of $15.7 billion (€12.3 billion) from the IMF itself and €6.5 billion ($8.4 billion) from the European Commission plus $1.3 billion (€1 billion) from the World Bank in a total loan package of $25.8 billion.[3] The quarterly reviews were completed as planned in February, May, September, November 2009 and February 2010. The EU

---

2. Paul Marer, "Global Crises and Eastern Europe," *Acta Oeconomica* 60, no. 1 (March): 30.

3. IMF, "IMF Executive Board Approves €12.3 Billion Stand-By Arrangement for Hungary," press release 08/275, November 6, 2008.

tranches were disbursed with similar regularity every fourth month, as the IMF program was meticulously adhered to.

The Hungarian fiscal stabilization was straightforward. The country's policy community knew what to do, and the crisis gave them a long-desired political mandate. Prime Minister Gyurcsány started the stabilization well, but he lacked the necessary authority. Hungary had reduced its budget deficit from 2006 to 2008 by raising revenues and cutting expenditures. On March 21, 2009, Gyurcsány was forced to resign as prime minister because of the opposition's virulent criticism of his ethics. In April, Gordon Bajnai, a businessman and technocrat, who was minister of national development and economy, took over as prime minister and executed strict stabilization.

The socialist party that stayed in government pursued a much more austere stabilization policy, keeping the budget deficit almost constant at 3.4 percent of GDP in 2008 and 3.9 percent of GDP in 2009. It was a broad-based policy trimming various expenditures (health care, education, public administration, pensions, and subsidies) and improving tax collection. At long last, the Hungarian government started slimming its exceedingly generous social transfer system and public employee compensation. Inevitably, capital expenditures were reduced. The already small subsidies were halved. The government reduced the payroll tax and tightened value-added taxation, moving taxes from labor to consumption. In spite of this rather strict stabilization during the global recession, GDP fell by comparatively limited 6.3 percent in 2009, and unexpectedly the Hungarian economy returned to growth in the first quarter of 2010. The constitutional court abolished two fiscal decisions by the government: property taxation and taxation of family allowances. Another complication was that state corporations repeatedly surprised with unexpected losses, which had to be financed by the treasury.[4]

The socialists' long incumbency and persistent accusations against them of corruption and the crisis led to a landslide victory of the center-right opposition Young Democrats under Viktor Orbán in April 2010. His government came in with a contradictory program of populism, structural reform, and stricter fiscal policies, but its policies have not settled as yet. The new government insists on introducing a flat personal income tax of 16 percent. Its negotiations with the IMF fell apart in July 2010, as the new government complained about the tight budget target (3.8 percent of GDP for 2010) agreed by the previous government. The Hungarian forint fell and bond yields rose on the news, but Hungary had actually not needed to draw the last two tranches of IMF funding. One reason for its

---

4. IMF, *Hungary: Fifth Review under the Stand-By Arrangement, and Request for Modification of Performance Criterion*, IMF Country Report No. 10/80 (Washington: International Monetary Fund, March 2010).

ignoring the IMF was that the government successfully raised the necessary budget financing by selling government bonds at reasonable prices. Yet the Hungarian government finally accepted the IMF demands.

Latvia: The Most Complex Stabilization

Of the CEE-10, Latvia's crisis was the most dramatic, complex, and interesting, as it was the most overheated economy and the stage for the main dispute between the IMF and the European Union over fixed exchange rates. Although the dispute primarily concerned Latvia, it also applied to the other three currency board countries, Lithuania, Estonia, and Bulgaria. Therefore, Latvia is worth considering in detail however small its economy is.

The Latvian economy had grown the fastest at an average of 9 percent a year in 2000–07, but its foreign debt reached 137 percent of GDP at the end of 2008. Its economic deceleration turned dramatic, as GDP plunged by 4.6 percent, and unemployment surged. The sudden contraction brought down state revenues, boosting the budget deficit to 4 percent of GDP in 2008.

In October 2008, the inability of Parex Bank to receive international financing stoked fear that Latvia would run out of foreign reserves and forced the government to go to the IMF. The IMF negotiations took about two months because of strife over whether Latvia should be forced to devalue and over complications with the Parex Bank, which was nationalized. Theoretically, three options existed: maintain a fixed exchange rate, freely floating exchange rate, or limited devaluation combined with unilateral introduction of the euro.

Latvia is an EU member and the European Union did not allow its members unilateral adoption of the euro, and Latvia did not want to forgo full membership of the EMU. Both the Latvian government and the people strongly opposed devaluation. As late as August 2009, an opinion poll reported that almost two-thirds of Latvians wanted the lat peg to the euro to remain unchanged.[5] They were prepared to do what it took, including large wage cuts, to keep the euro peg and adopt the euro early. The government was committed to complying with the fiscal Maastricht criteria by 2012 and adopting the euro by 2014. The Latvian alternative to devaluation was called "internal devaluation," which meant large cost and wage cuts.

If devaluation had been undertaken, it would probably have been sharp, because lats are used for little but tax payments, public expenditures, wage payments, and retail trade. Of all domestic credit, 87 percent was in euro, while more assets were in lats. An uncontrolled depreciation

---

5. IMF External Relations Department, *Morning Press*, August 4, 2009.

on a very thin market could easily have amounted to 50 percent, devastating Latvia's finances, as the country's foreign debt would have doubled to some 270 percent of GDP. With mortgages predominantly in euro, depreciation would have led to an avalanche of bad debt and mortgage defaults, which would have aggravated output contraction, and the sharp devaluation would have boosted inflation. The strained banking system would have collapsed. Given that Latvia is a small, open economy, the positive effect would have been comparatively limited, which would have aggravated the depreciation. The pass-through of inflation would probably have been so large that Latvia would have been unable to fulfill the Maastricht criterion for inflation for years.

In the end, the IMF accepted that Latvia not devalue. Christoph Rosenberg, who led the December 2008 IMF mission to Latvia, laid out the arguments against devaluation. The key reason was that this was the Latvian choice.[6] The IMF was also persuaded by the substantial financing of the European Union and the Nordic countries, which supported the Latvian choice. The total stabilization package amounted to €7.5 billion ($10.5 billion). For a country with a GDP of only $28 billion in 2008, this was more than one-third its GDP. The IMF provided more financing than usual, €1.7 billion ($2.37 billion) or 12 times Latvia's quota, but only 23 percent of the total package. As a virtuous member of the European Union, Latvia could count on European support: The European Union contributed €3.1 billion ($4.3 billion), the Nordic countries €1.8 billion ($2.5 billion), the World Bank €400 million, the Czech Republic €200 million, and the EBRD, Estonia, and Poland €100 million each.[7] Latvia's extreme openness necessitated such assistance. Its smallness and virtues made this massive support possible. Yet it was clearly stated that the multilateral support should be used first and the bilateral support only if needed. The interest rate of the multilateral credits was about 3.5 percent a year, while the bilateral credits would have cost close to 6 percent a year. As of June 2010, Latvia had not drawn on any bilateral financing.

Latvia's politics are fragmented, with the government usually changing every year (as in the other Baltic countries), but the government is always a coalition of four to five ethnically Latvian center-right parties. On October 7, 2006, Latvia held its last parliamentary elections before the crisis, with seven parties passing the 5 percent hurdle to enter parliament. Traditionally, three of these parties were "owned" by an oligarch, while two parties represented the Russian minority, but one, New Era, was a Latvian free-market and anticorruption party. One four-party center-right coalition collapsed in December 2007 due to strife over anticorruption action.

---

6. Christoph Rosenberg, "Why the IMF Supports the Latvian Currency Peg," *RGE Monitor*, January 6, 2009.

7. IMF, "IMF Announces Staff-Level Agreement with Latvia on a €1.7 Billion Stand-By Arrangement," press release 08/332, December 19, 2008.

An anticrisis government of similar composition was formed under former prime minister Ivars Godmanis, who concluded the IMF agreement. Minister of Finance Atis Slakteris aroused public fury in December, when in a Bloomberg television interview he was asked about the causes of the crisis in Latvia and responded in broken English: "Nothing special." On January 13, 2009, riots broke out in Riga, leading to a political crisis that prompted Godmanis' resignation in February. A new five-party coalition government was formed, led by New Era, the anticorruption and free-market party, whose young leader and former minister of finance Valdis Dombrovskis became prime minister. Although two oligarchic parties participated in the coalition, Latvia had a government that was even more determined to solve the crisis.

In early June 2009, Latvia experienced a few days of a last devaluation scare. The IMF was supposed to issue its second tranche in March 2009, but it was dissatisfied with Latvia's fiscal performance, as the crisis undermined state revenues and boosted social expenditures, and it questioned Latvia's statistics. Meanwhile the Latvian government was reluctant to announce the necessary measures before the local and European elections in early June.

The country went through two major rounds of fiscal consolidation. The first package of December 2008 focused on reductions in public wages of 20 percent, an increase in the value-added tax (VAT) from 18 to 21 percent, and hikes in excise taxes. Altogether, this package was supposed to amount to 7 percent of GDP, compared with the budget passed in November, but much of it was not implemented because of the unexpectedly severe recession. In April 2009, state pension contributions were reduced.

In June 2009, the Latvian government had to accept a second package of fiscal tightening of an additional 4 percent of GDP.[8] Now it launched another major anticrisis program, cutting public salaries a second time by 20 percent to a total of 35 percent, with the actual total assessed at 25 to 30 percent; the public administration was slashed by 20 percent, with a total reduction of 14,000 public jobs.[9] Half of all government agencies were eliminated. Latvia had a ratio of one teacher for every six students, the highest in Europe. This country of 2.3 million people had far too many hospitals, a Soviet inheritance of more hospital beds than medical care. It closed 24 of 49 hospitals to the benefit of public health. Public pensions were reduced by 10 percent.[10] Eventually, the Latvian parliament adopted

---

8. European Commission, "Cross-Country Study: Economic Policy Changes in the Baltics," *European Economy*, Occasional Papers 58 (Brussels, February 2010), 68.

9. "The Lex Column: Greece/Latvia," *Financial Times*, May 7, 2010.

10. Interview with Prime Minister Valdis Dombrovskis in Riga, June 5, 2010.

all these measures, but the Latvian constitutional court reversed the pension cuts as unconstitutional.

After these budget cuts, the new Latvian government assessed its likely budget deficit at 9 percent of GDP. The European Commission hesitantly concurred, but the IMF believed it might be as large as 15.5 percent of GDP, although Latvia had a strong tradition of nearly balanced budgets and minimal public debt. Eventually, the actual budget deficit did turn out to be 9 percent of GDP. The Europeans started wondering why the IMF had not yet disbursed the money. On July 2, the European Union went ahead on its own, giving Latvia a huge second tranche of $1.7 billion, which marked the end of the acute Latvian financial crisis.

Finally, on July 27, a doubtful IMF decided to disburse a second tranche.[11] The Bank of Latvia was no longer forced to intervene to support the lat. Credit default swap rates and interest rates continued to fall and normalized by September. In August, annualized inflation had dropped to 1.8 percent from 15 percent a year earlier, as prices were falling every month. In October 2009, the IMF and European Union demanded another round of public expenditure cuts of 1.5 percent of GDP for 2010, which brought the last wind of crisis. Latvia's total fiscal adjustment in 2009 was probably 10 percent of GDP. From September 2009, interest rates and other financial conditions started normalizing.

In March 2010, one of the oligarchic parties in the five-party coalition departed from the government but it continued ruling with minority support in parliament. Legislation has come to a near halt until parliamentary election in October 2010. First to have started contracting in the region, Latvia is likely to return to economic growth last—in the fourth quarter of 2010.

Romania: All About Politics

The case of Romania was all about politics. It needed an IMF program because of its problems rolling over its limited public debt, but not as badly as Hungary and Latvia. Therefore, the IMF moved cautiously, afraid of being caught up in the complex domestic politics and finding it difficult to receive credible government decisions.

After long deliberations the IMF and Romania concluded a two-year standby agreement on March 25, 2009, of $17.1 billion (€12.95 billion). The whole package, including financing from the European Commission (€5 billion or $6.5 billion) and the World Bank, amounted to $27 billion

---

11. IMF, "IMF Reaches Staff-Level Agreement with the Latvian Authorities on First Review under Stand-by Arrangement," press release, July 27, 2009.

(€20 billion).[12] Both the IMF and the European Union moved slowly because of the political turmoil. Each made a disbursement in the second quarter of 2009, but the collapse of the government in October and the presidential elections in November and December forced them to take a break.

With disputes over corruption, politics became very nasty, including a failed attempt to impeach center-right and anticorruption campaigner President Traian Băsescu in the spring of 2007. Parliamentary elections on November 30, 2008, ended in near deadlock with the center-right Democratic Liberal Party and the Social Democratic Party, which each received roughly one-third of the votes. The liberal democrats and social democrats formed a coalition after the election. President Băsescu opposed one liberal democratic candidate and eventually nominated another, Emil Boc, as prime minister. The Social Democratic Party pulled out of the coalition government in October 2009, leaving liberal democratic Prime Minister Boc with a minority government, which lost a confidence vote in parliament, as members of parliament criticized Boc's failure to pull the country out of recession.

In December 2009, Băsescu was narrowly reelected as president in a runoff against a social democrat. He asked Boc to form a new coalition government, and a functioning government was finally in place in January 2010 with a like-minded president and prime minister. The government quickly introduced stringent budget cuts and vowed to address the country's financial crisis. The IMF rapidly undertook both second and third reviews and the European Commission followed suit. Romania's large current account deficit of 12.2 percent of GDP in 2008 contracted to 4.4 percent in 2009. The budget deficit that rose to 8.3 percent of GDP in 2009 is expected to moderate to 6.5 percent of GDP in 2010.

In May 2010, however, Romania was hit by contagion from the Greek crisis, and the government preempted by cutting public salaries by 25 percent and pensions by 15 percent. This time large but peaceful demonstrations erupted. However, the Romanian constitutional court vetoed the pension cuts, which compelled the government to raise the VAT instead by 5 percentage points. In August 2010, Romania concluded negotiations on its sixth IMF tranche and its third EU tranche. Economic growth is expected to reemerge during the second half of 2010.

While Romania's governments have shifted, Mugur Isărescu has been governor of the National Bank of Romania since 1990 apart from a brief interlude as prime minister in 1999–2000. As Romania's leading economic policymaker, Isărescu has been a stabilizing factor, though for many years Romania had the highest inflation in Eastern Europe.

---

12. "IMF Executive Board Approves €12.9 Billion Stand-By Arrangement for Romania," press release no. 09/148, May 4, 2009.

Lithuania, Estonia, and Bulgaria: Robust Anticrisis Policy without the IMF

It is natural to discuss the three countries with full-fledged currency boards—Lithuania, Estonia, and Bulgaria—in one context. All three stand out for their orthodox crisis resolution and none of them required IMF support in spite of large current account deficits.

Most remarkable was that **Lithuania** did not need an IMF program. Its economic situation was strikingly similar to Latvia's, with a current account deficit of 13 percent of GDP in 2008, but it escaped the initial crisis, as it was less overheated and had no large collapsing domestic bank. Its foreign debt was only 69 percent of GDP at the end of 2008.

Its politics differed from Latvia's. Lithuania had a strong postcommunist Social Democratic Party and its politics were neither oligarchic nor ethnic, as ethnic Lithuanians comprised an overwhelming majority. The social democrats were governing when the crisis hit. The October 2008 parliamentary elections delivered a victory to the conservative Homeland Union, whose leader, Andrius Kubilius, became prime minister in November. A center-right coalition government was formed, and it was determined to salvage Lithuania. Kubilius, a man of great calm, was at ease with the crisis. He had been prime minister in the aftermath of the Russian financial crisis in 1999–2000, which gave him credibility. Soon after he assumed office, however, Vilnius faced violent riots on January 14, 2009. Kubilius brushed them off, and they were not repeated, as Lithuanians were shocked by the violence. He was the ultimate fiscal hawk, stating: "My advice would be simple: start fiscal consolidation as soon as possible."[13]

Having seen the negative publicity Latvia received from its IMF negotiations, Kubilius was determined to avoid the IMF. Nor did he want to risk the fixed exchange rate. His plan was as simple as radical: to cut public expenditures by 8 percent of GDP in 2009 and an additional 5 percent of GDP in 2010.[14] The first fiscal consolidation of 4 percent of GDP was adopted in December 2008. It contained a comprehensive tax reform and broad expenditure cuts, coupled with reductions in the mandatory pension fund. In May 2009, a second package was adopted of about 3 percent of GDP, focusing on more expenditure cuts, less generous health insurance, and smaller pension fund contributions. In a July 2009 package of 0.5 percent of GDP, VAT was raised by 1 percentage point.[15]

---

13. Andrew Ward, "Baltic Trio Shows How Fiscal Medicine Tastes," *Financial Times*, June 25, 2010.

14. Personal interview with Andrius Kubilius in October 2009.

15. European Commission, "Cross-Country Study," 68.

Lithuania overperformed and cut expenditures by 8.6 percent of GDP in 2009, but even so the sharply falling revenues led to a budget deficit of 8.9 percent of GDP. It undertook serious public-sector reforms, initiating a radical reform of higher education.

Lithuania continued to borrow on the eurobond market as required throughout the crisis. In early June 2009, when Latvia went through a bout of devaluation speculation, its yields peaked at 9.5 percent per annum, but by October the yields had fallen to 6.8 percent per annum and then normalized. Its GDP fell by 15 percent in 2009, but its current account swung to a surplus of 3.2 percent of GDP. Economic growth returned in the second quarter of 2010. Like Latvia, Lithuania has had to postpone its plans for adoption of the euro until 2014, but its determination is intact.

Estonia has all along been the most radical market reformer in Europe.[16] As in Latvia and Lithuania, each government lasted about one year, but they had all been similar center-right coalition governments, excluding both socialists and the Russian minority. Because of solid free-market orientation, the political shade of the government made little difference. The parliamentary elections of March 4, 2007, resulted in a typical center-right coalition under Prime Minister Andrus Ansip, probably more free market than any other government in Europe. Like its predecessors, the government was profoundly fiscally conservative and aimed at the earliest adoption of the euro, although Estonia had a huge current account deficit of 18 percent of GDP in 2007 and a foreign debt of 114 percent of GDP.

The world at large considered Estonia to be in deep financial crisis and speculated whether it would be forced to devalue or accept an IMF program, but neither the people nor the government recognized any crisis. They focused on fulfilling all Maastricht criteria to join the EMU in January 2011. The Estonian GDP declined by 3.6 percent in 2008 and 14 percent in 2009, but with an average annual growth of 8.2 percent during the preceding eight years, the Estonians did not complain. The government assessed its austerity measures, mainly budget cuts, at more than 9 percent of GDP.[17] The persistent budget surpluses were interrupted with a minor deficit of 2.7 percent of GDP in 2008 and 1.7 percent of GDP in 2009, but Estonia was probably undertaking the most radical fiscal cuts of all countries. In 2009, its public debt was minuscule at 6.4 percent of GDP. Thus, Estonia complied with all the Maastricht criteria.

Estonia has already returned to growth, and the public remains convinced that their government was right to stick to the currency board, pursue a strict fiscal policy, and maintain the freest economy in Europe.

---

16. Mart Laar, *Little Country That Could* (London: Centre for Research into Post-Communist Economies, 2002).

17. Ott Ummelas, "Estonian GDP Shrinks on Low Spending, Investments," *Bloomberg Businessweek*, May 11, 2010.

Estonia has been approved by the European Union for euro adoption in January 2011. The Ansip free-market government sat unthreatened. Like Poland and the Czech Republic, Estonia participated in the financial support package for Latvia in December 2008.

Bulgaria was most remarkable in escaping the crisis, although most indicators presaged a serious crisis: Its current account deficit was 24 percent of GDP in 2008, its foreign debt exceeded GDP, and inflation was 12 percent in 2008. But even so GDP declined by a moderate 5.1 percent in 2009. Bulgaria's good performance is paradoxical. Two explanations are persistent budget surpluses of 3 to 3.5 percent of GDP in 2006–08 and huge foreign direct investment that financed the whole current account deficit. It recorded an insignificant budget deficit of 0.8 percent of GDP in 2009.

Strangely, Bulgaria's politics have been reminiscent of the Baltics with almost annual changes of coalition governments, but it has had a strong postcommunist socialist party (as Romania and Hungary), and the country has seen big swings between socialists and conservatives. After the elections in 2005, seven different party blocs were represented in parliament. At the time of the crisis a fiscally responsible socialist coalition was leading the country.

In July 2009, parliamentary elections brought in a more economically responsible minority government under Prime Minister Boyko Borisov. He headed the new party Citizens for European Development and had made his name as an anticorruption fighter. His government opted for an even stricter anticrisis policy than its socialist predecessor with three main aims: combat corruption, rein in the budget deficit, and maintain the currency board. It has focused on cutting the public administration.

However, it was in for a rude surprise. The former government had left public procurement contracts of about 2 percent of GDP off the books. In response, the Bulgarian government decided to cut spending on the public sector by one-fifth.[18] Contrary to what a cursory reader of statistics would have thought, Bulgaria sailed through the crisis with little suffering.

Poland, the Czech Republic, Slovakia, and Slovenia: No Serious Overheating or Crisis

The four remaining CEE-10 countries did not experience any real overheating and were very different from the other CEE-10 countries. Slovenia had adopted the euro in January 2007 and Slovakia in January 2009.

Before the crisis their economic policies had differed greatly from those of the currency board countries. Slovakia, the Czech Republic, and

---

18. "Bulgaria Fiscal Position: Government to Cut Public Spending by One Fifth," RGE Critical Issue, May 10, 2010, www.roubini.com.

Poland all accepted a nominal effective exchange rate appreciation of 30 to 40 percent from the beginning of 2003 until the onset of the crisis in the third quarter of 2008.[19] As a consequence, these countries had stable and moderate monetary expansion (figure 2.8), and their inflation stayed below 3 percent in 2007.

Since Slovenia had the euro and Slovakia was about to obtain it, both benefited from European Central Bank (ECB) liquidity, and they were not subject to the same credit crunch as the other East Europeans. The Czech Republic and Poland went through big depreciation during the first half year of liquidity squeeze, but they came through without serious effects.

Consequently, public confidence was not really shaken, and domestic demand, which was the main force driving down GDP in the region, fell little. In 2007, none of these four countries had a budget deficit of more than 2 percent of GDP, so they were not forced to austerity in the midst of the crisis but could allow themselves budget deficits of 5.5 to 6.8 percent of GDP in 2009 in a reasonable countercyclical policy. Yet, in 2010, concerns have been raised about Poland, the Czech Republic, and Slovenia that they are too relaxed, not trying to control their structural budget deficits as are all the other countries in the region.

Under these conditions, the politics and color of their governments made little difference. Poland and the Czech Republic had center-right governments, while Slovakia and Slovenia had social democratic governments. Neither evidenced any strong ideological course, though the center-right won a big victory in the Czech Republic in May 2010 and a small victory in Slovakia one month later.

Fast Financial Adjustment

Throughout the region, economic adjustment was swift. Seldom has the world seen such rapid changes in the current account. The swing was greatest in Latvia, which went from a current account deficit of 13 percent of GDP in 2008 to a surplus of 9.4 percent in 2009—no less than 22 percent of GDP in a single year. Estonia and Lithuania also shifted from big deficits to significant surpluses, while most other CEE-10 countries ended up close to balance. Only Bulgaria maintained a large current account deficit of 9.5 percent of GDP, financed by continued large foreign direct investment (figure 3.1).

Inflation fell sharply in the deflationary climate of the global recession with minimal credit issue. The change was most extreme in the Baltic countries, where credit had expanded by about 50 percent a year in 2006

19. Bas B. Bakker and Anne-Marie Gulde, "The Credit Boom in the EU New Member States: Bad Luck or Bad Policies?" IMF Working Paper 10/130 (Washington: International Monetary Fund, 2010), 35.

Figure 3.1 Current account balance, 2008–09

percent of GDP

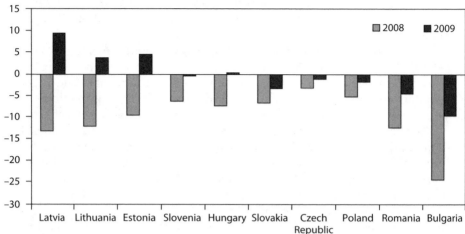

Source: IMF, *World Economic Outlook,* April 2010, www.imf.org (accessed on April 30, 2010).

and 2007, but started shrinking in 2009, resulting in deflation in Latvia and Lithuania. Most of the other CEE-10 countries will probably have 2 percent inflation or less, and only Hungary and Romania are likely to have about 4 percent inflation in 2010 (figure 3.2). This is the chance for all these countries to seize control of their price development.

Budget deficits increased because of the crisis, but not as much as in Western Europe. The average unweighted budget deficit of the CEE-10 rose from 3 percent of GDP in 2008 to 6 percent of GDP in 2009 and is expected to contract to 5 percent of GDP in 2010. This stands in stark contrast to the PIGS (Portugal, Italy, Greece, and Spain), where budget deficits swelled to 11 percent of GDP in 2009 (figure 3.3).

Public expenditures rose as a share of GDP. Before the crisis, the EU-15 had average public expenditures of 46 to 47 percent of GDP. Central Europe had almost as high public expenditures, but the average was boosted by Hungary. The three Baltic states saw their public expenditures rise as a share of GDP from 35 percent in 2007 to 44 percent in 2009, while Central Europe experienced a marginal rise to 46 percent of GDP, leaving Southeastern Europe with the lowest public expenditures (figure 3.4). In the crisis year of 2009, public expenditure as a share of GDP rose sharply because of contracting GDP, rising pension costs, and other social costs related to rising unemployment. The East Europeans largely abstained from state aid so common in Western Europe during the crisis.

Yet all these countries cut their public expenditures substantially—the

Figure 3.2   Inflation, 2009 and 2010e

average consumer prices (percent)

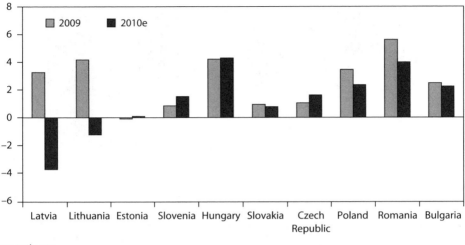

e = estimate

Source: IMF, *World Economic Outlook* database, www.imf.org (accessed on August 10, 2010).

Baltics by as much as 8 to 10 percent of GDP in 2009 alone, but revenues fell much more. By 2012, most of the CEE-10 countries aim at fulfilling the Maastricht budget criterion of a maximum budget deficit of 3 percent of GDP, which means they are planning very tight fiscal policies for 2010–12. Even so, the East Europeans have by and large bought the idea that it is better to cut expenditures than to raise taxes. Alberto Alesina and Silvia Ardagna offer substantial statistical evidence for the thesis that "fiscal adjustments...based upon spending cuts and no tax increases are more likely to reduce deficits and debt over GDP ratios than those based upon tax increases."[20]

The reduction in public expenditures has not been even. The big cuts have concentrated on public administration and public wages. Subsidies and capital expenditures have also been reduced, as is usually the case in crises. Two big innovative reforms have been those of the health care system in Latvia and of higher education in Lithuania. The overall trend in social service reforms has been to pay for services provided and not for existing real estate and staff.

Pensions have presented big and peculiar problems. Pension expenditures have been large and retirement ages low, with many categories

20. Alberto F. Alesina and Silvia Ardagna, "Large Changes in Fiscal Policy: Taxes Versus Spending," NBER Working Paper 15438 (Cambridge, MA: National Bureau of Economic Research, 2009).

Figure 3.3   Average budget deficit, CEE-10 and PIGS, 2008–10e

percent of GDP

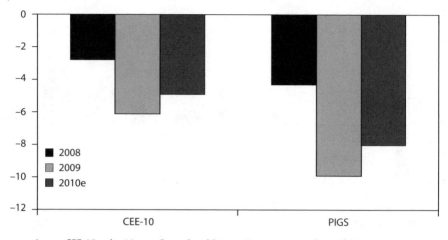

e = estimate; CEE-10 = the 10 new Central and Eastern European members of the European Union; PIGS = Portugal, Italy, Greece, and Spain

Source: Eurostat database, http://epp.eurostat.ec.europa.eu (accessed on April 22, 2010); author's calculations.

Figure 3.4   Total general government expenditure, CEE-10 and EU-15, 2004–11f

percent of GDP

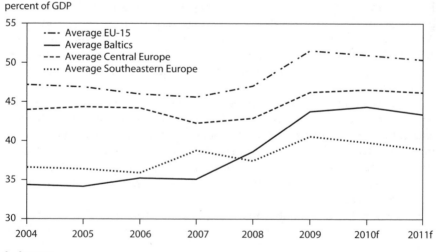

f = forecast

Sources: Eurostat database, http://epp.eurostat.ec.europa.eu (accessed on May 4, 2010); Directorate General for Economic and Financial Affairs, European Commission, European Economic Forecast—Spring 2010, *European Economy* 2 (May 2010), provisional version, p. 199.

receiving early retirement but low pensions. Some trimming of social transfers has taken place, but pensions have been shielded by the constitutional courts in Latvia and Romania. In Latvia, which suffered the biggest output contraction, pensions as a share of GDP rose from 6 to 10 percent, since they were not reduced. A conflict has arisen between pension reforms aimed at building up private mandatory pension funds based on savings and the financing of public pensions. By and large, the public pension funds won against the private ones.[21] Naturally, as unemployment is rising, a tightening of pension rules is inconvenient, but after the crisis has passed, pension reform is one of the big items on the reform agenda. Retirement ages must be raised and early pensions sharply reduced. Funded pension insurance needs to be revived.

Taxation has gone through substantial structural changes. State revenues have fallen even more than GDP during the crisis but still have held up reasonably well. Taxation has moved from labor and capital to consumption, while tax bases have been broadened. Many countries have raised excise taxes and eliminated loopholes in the VAT. The three real crisis countries, Latvia, Hungary, and Romania, have all been forced to raise their VAT by a few percent.[22] Property taxes were raised in a few countries, notably Latvia and Romania, but the Romanian constitutional court aborted the Romanian property tax.

By contrast, not a single CEE-10 country has raised its personal income taxes, and no fewer than seven of the CEE-10 have flat income taxes, ranging from 10 percent in Bulgaria to 23 percent in Latvia. The Czech Republic introduced its flat income tax of 15 percent in 2008, and the new Hungarian government plans to adopt a flat income tax of 16 percent in 2011. In spite of the crisis, Latvia reduced its flat income tax from 25 to 23 percent in January 2009. Payroll and social security taxes have been reduced slightly. Similarly, corporate profit taxes remain very low, and several countries decreased them further as a stimulus during the crisis, though Lithuania went against the tide and raised its corporate profit tax from 15 to 20 percent in 2009.[23] Thus, both on the income side and on the expenditure side, the East European countries have undertaken substantial structural improvement, which will likely lead to greater economic efficiency in the future.

Foreign indebtedness has risen as almost all foreign claims coming due have been refinanced and GDP has fallen. Eastern Europe's deep inte-

---

21. European Commission, "Cross-Country Study," 68; Leszek Kostrzewski and Piotr Miączynński, "Emerytura później i biedniej (Pension later and poorer)," *Gazeta wyborcza*, June 8, 2010, 2.

22. Latvia raised VAT from 18 to 21 percent, Hungary from 20 to 21 percent, and Romania from 19 to 24 percent.

23. European Commission, *Taxation Trends in the European Union: Data for the EU Member States and Norway* (Luxembourg: European Communities, 2009).

gration was perceived as an insurance policy before the crisis. In the midst of the crisis, that appeared to be an illusion, but in 2009 the deep financial integration worked out. Not a single West European bank sold or closed any subsidiary in any East European country, and declines in exports were very limited in comparison with those of Russia or East Asia.

For economic output, 2009 delivered a shock. Latvia's GDP is likely to contract by a total of 25 percent in 2008–10, but that is less than the 33 percent growth in Latvian GDP in 2005–07. The two countries with the next biggest output falls are Estonia and Lithuania with 17 to 18 percent decline in the course of two years. Then come several other CEE-10 countries with total contractions of 5 to 7 percent, which is not all too dramatic in the global Great Recession and in the same league as many Western countries.

As is usually the case in a severe financial crisis, most of the contraction came from decline in domestic demand for both investment and consumption, which contracted by no less than 24 to 28 percent in the three Baltic countries. Once the people calm down from their worst panic, these countries should be able to recover fast, as their current accounts have swung to large surpluses. Surprisingly, in 2009 Slovakia and the Czech Republic experienced a greater contraction of their exports than the Baltics, by 16 percent compared with 11 to 15.5 percent.[24] The export structure turned out to be more important than the exchange rate.

As of the second quarter of 2010, economic growth had resumed in all CEE-10 countries but Latvia and Romania, which will return to growth in the fourth quarter of 2010. The region as a whole lost two to three years of economic growth, which is no catastrophe considering the growth the region enjoyed from 2000 until 2008. Nobody seriously claims to have disinvented the business cycle, and recessions remain necessary to cleanse the capitalist economy from temporary excesses. Most important are long-term economic growth and social development.

Total GDP growth from 2000 to 2010 (with IMF growth forecasts for 2010) offers a rather intriguing picture (figure 3.5). The average decade-long growth for the CEE-10 was 42 percent, which is respectable but not impressive. Slovakia with 60 percent growth is the undisputed leader. It was a reform laggard in the 1990s but around 2004 it undertook the most radical market reforms in Central Europe in the 2000s, and it introduced the euro with a sensible exchange rate in January 2009. Romania being number two is perhaps most astonishing, but it represents the most obvious catch-up case, since it did the least reform in the 1990s.

Four of the next five CEE-10 countries have currency boards, indicating why their populations defended them so firmly in the crisis. Materially, they did not suffer much over the last decade even if 2009 was rough. Poland, which has been a star during the crisis, comes in the middle

24. Bakker and Gulde, "The Credit Boom in the EU New Member States," 22.

Figure 3.5 Total GDP growth, 2000–10f

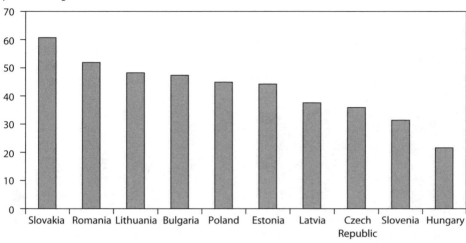

f = forecast

Source: IMF, *World Economic Outlook,* April 2010, www.imf.org (accessed on May 7, 2010).

because of its low growth in the early 2000s, when it brought inflation and an excessive fiscal deficit under control.

The three growth laggards offer no surprises: Hungary (22 percent), Slovenia (31 percent), and the Czech Republic (36 percent). They had the highest GDP per capita to begin with and had carried out extensive structural reforms in the early 1990s, benefiting less than the others from catch-up or economic convergence growth in the 2000s. Hungary has persistently sinned against all fiscal rules, for which it has been punished with low growth. Slovenia has undertaken no new reforms, so why should it grow fast? If we combine the 1990s and the 2000s, the overall picture is one of common economic growth and convergence with the European Union.

Eastern Europe is converging with Western Europe but not all that fast. During the 15 years from 1993 until 2008, the average GDP per capita measured in purchasing power parity rose from just over one-third of the level of the old EU-15 (36.6 percent) to half that level (50.6 percent), an increase by 38.5 percent. Every single eastern EU country had risen substantially relative to the EU-15. Yet only the two wealthiest countries (Slovenia and the Czech Republic) had overtaken Portugal, the poorest of the old EU members, and Slovenia's GDP per capita was only 78 percent of the EU-15 level (figure 3.6). Among all countries in the world in 2008, Slovenia ranked 32nd, the Czech Republic 37th, while Estonia, Hungary, Lithuania, Poland, and Latvia followed at 43rd to 49th, Romania 58th, and Bulgaria 68th.

Figure 3.6   GDP per capita in the CEE-10 as share of average EU-15 GDP per capita

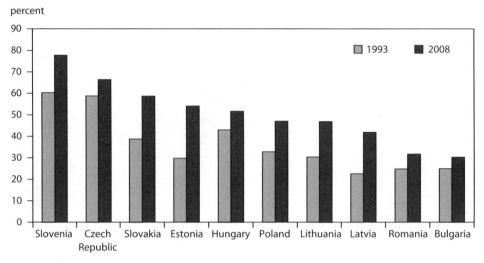

PPP = purchasing power parity

Note: GDP per capita in PPP (constant 2005 international dollars) as a share of average EU-15 GDP per capita in PPP.

Source: World Bank, *World Development Indicators* online database (accessed on August 9, 2010).

The greatest social concern has been unemployment, which usually peaks slightly after growth resumes. For the region as a whole, unemployment seems to have peaked in the first quarter of 2010 and then leveled out. Not surprisingly, Latvia recorded the highest unemployment in the region at 20 percent, while Estonia followed with 19 percent, Lithuania 17 percent, Slovakia with 15 percent, and Hungary at 11 percent, while the other five countries have unemployment below the EU average of 9.5 percent. The gravest concern that these figures raise is that the three Baltic states may face a serious threat of emigration. Their populations have already declined by about 15 percent since independence in 1991. Yet, all three countries have seen an early fall in unemployment in the first half of 2010.

The wage picture remains murky. Public wages have officially been cut by up to 35 percent in Latvia, by 25 percent in Romania, and substantially in several other countries. Yet, the overall public wage declines as recorded in public statistics have been much less. Private-sector wages have also fallen, but by much less. Yet, anecdotal evidence suggests that they might have decreased more than statistics reveal, because many unofficial perks have been the first to go. Large private wage cuts of 15 to 20 percent appear to be common and easily accepted. It appears as if high-salaried staff has faced the largest cuts, because this segment of the labor market was most overheated. Therefore, the recession might have had an equalizing effect, which might have contributed to the social calm.

The crisis has forced all CEE-10 countries to trim their public sectors and improve their economic systems, which will render them even more competitive. Most factors point to renewed, sound economic growth, though it will be constrained by less credit expansion because of deleveraging and slow economic growth in Western Europe, the dominant export market of Eastern Europe. Free-market policies are not in danger, nor are democracy or social peace. After a decade of very high economic growth, these countries encountered their first serious recession, but they took it on the chin. The big issue that remains to be resolved is the exchange rate and monetary regime.

4

The Exchange Rate Dilemma

"The greatest pleasure in life is doing what people say you cannot do."
—Walter Bagehot, *Lombard Street*, 1873

The East European countries were attractive for foreign investment because of their successful transition to market economies, low production costs, and access to the European market. The whole region was characterized by great openness to both foreign trade and finance. But why did some, and not all, countries end up with too large current account deficits, foreign debts, credit expansion, and inflation?

The central cause of the region's financial crisis was the long-lasting expansionary monetary policy of the US Federal Reserve and other central banks, notably the European Central Bank (ECB), which exposed the East European nations to a flood of credit. The ECB had one mandate: to target inflation. It did so aptly, keeping it almost exactly at an average of 2 percent a year. However, the accusations of exceedingly loose monetary policy that have been made against the US Federal Reserve can also be directed against the ECB in the run-up to the financial crisis. In the four years 2005–08, money supply (M2) in the eurozone increased by an average of 9.5 percent a year. In most of the eurozone, a massive real estate boom took place, especially in Spain and Ireland, but the ECB found no reason to lean against the wind. A sizable carry trade transferred credit to Eastern and Southern Europe.

The question for policymakers in Eastern Europe was how to shield their country from the eurozone's overflow of short-term capital and its inflationary effects. There were three methods: inflation targeting with exchange rate appreciation and tight monetary policy, bank regulation, and fiscal surpluses.

The crucial policy choice was the exchange rate.[1] The CEE-10 countries pursued three different exchange rate regimes: floating exchange rates, euro, and currency boards. Four were inflation targeters with a floating exchange rate: Poland and the Czech Republic targeted inflation in the most orthodox fashion, while Hungary and Romania intervened moderately. The former two were successful, but the latter two needed International Monetary Fund (IMF) programs.

Two countries adopted the euro, Slovenia and Slovakia (in 2007 and 2009, respectively). They escaped capital flight and the liquidity freeze, as the ECB guaranteed their financial stability and liquidity, but their production costs became disproportionately high relative to competitors, such as Poland and the Czech Republic, that undertook large devaluations.

The third group consisted of the four countries with currency boards and fixed exchange rates: the three Baltic states and Bulgaria. The Baltic countries had fixed their exchange rates to escape the postcommunist crisis in 1992–94 and Bulgaria did the same to combat its brief hyperinflation in 1997. In all four countries, the currency boards worked well as nominal anchors. They minimized fiscal deficits, brought down high inflation, provided a transparent monetary regime, and supported high economic growth.[2] "Fixed exchange rate regimes have been a central element of the Baltic model since transition: credible pegs fostered policy discipline and were among the attractive features for foreign investors."[3]

Estonia and Bulgaria had steady budget surpluses, while Latvia and Lithuania maintained almost balanced budgets. The currency boards had proven themselves by holding during the Russian financial crisis in 1998. However, these countries were worst hit by the financial crisis, since they received no support from the ECB, while the currency boards lacked credibility with foreign investors. Yet, only Latvia needed an IMF program, whereas Estonia and Bulgaria were helped by their persistent large fiscal surpluses. Remarkably, none of these countries has devalued, and politically the currency board remains a sacred cow in each of these countries, ardently supported by a large popular majority.

---

1. For a broad overview and discussion of exchange rate policy in transition countries, see Balázs Égert, László Halpern, and Ronald MacDonald, "Equilibrium Exchange Rates in Transition Economies: Taking Stock of the Issues," *Journal of Economic Surveys* 20, no. 2 (2006): 257–324.

2. Steve H. Hanke, Lars Jonung, and Kurt Schuler, *Monetary Reform for a Free Estonia: A Currency Board Solution* (Stockholm: SNS Förlag, 1992); Ardo H. Hansson and Jeffrey D. Sachs, "Crowning the Estonian kroon," *Transition* 3, no. 9: 1–3 (Washington: World Bank, 1992); John Williamson, *What Role for Currency Boards?* (Washington: Institute for International Economics, 1995).

3. Servaas Deroose, Elena Flores, Gabriele Giudice, and Alessandro Turrini, "The Tale of the Baltics: Experiences, challenges Ahead and Main Lessons," *ECFIN Economic Brief* no. 10 (European Commission, July 2010), 8.

Kosovo and Montenegro, which are outside the European Union and the scope of this study, adopted the euro unilaterally. This gave greater credibility to their economies than to the currency board countries. The euro itself had this stabilizing effect, as the ECB did not grant these countries any financial support.

Poland stands out as the greatest success in the crisis, being the only EU country to grow in 2009. Thanks to a floating exchange rate and strict banking supervision, its capital inflows were comparatively limited. The National Bank of Poland (NBP) pursued strict inflation targeting and kept inflation low by maintaining positive real interest rates when most other countries failed to do so. The NBP leaned against the wind when it perceived that asset prices, notably housing prices, were rising too steeply. Unlike other East European countries, Poland regulated the volume of mortgages in foreign currency.[4] With its strict monetary policy, when Leszek Balcerowicz headed the NBP (2001–07), Poland could get away with a comparatively large budget deficit.

The Czech Republic pursued a similar policy, and Slovakia had a managed float without explicit inflation targeting until it entered the European Exchange Rate Mechanism (ERM II) in November 2005 to adopt the euro in January 2009. Sebastian Edwards' overall judgment of inflation targeting stands: "Countries that have adopted [inflation targeting] have experienced" less pass-through "from exchange rate changes to inflation." However, his other conclusion that inflation targeting "has not resulted in an increase in (nominal or real) exchange rate volatility" did not hold at the height of the crisis, when exchange rate volatility became extreme even for well-managed economies.[5]

The countries with currency boards faced the Impossible Trinity: With fixed exchange rates and free capital movements (stipulated by EU membership), they could not pursue an independent monetary policy. Their interest rates were set by the market, but in effect determined by the Economic and Monetary Union (EMU), leaving their nominal interest rates too low and real interest rates negative. Even if these countries had been able to hike their interest rates, the effect would not have been monetary contraction but further attraction of short-term foreign capital, given the fixed exchange rate.

Eventually, the long-lasting credit expansion superseded the rising

4. Leszek Balcerowicz, "Is the Present Crisis the Moment for the Euro's Global Emergence?" Panel discussion with Antonio de Lecea, Leszek Balcerowicz, C. Fred Bergsten, Erkki Liikanen, and Lawrence H. Summers, in *The Euro at Ten: The Next Global Currency?* eds. Jean Pisani-Ferry and Adam S. Posen (Washington: Peterson Institute for International Economics, 2009), 193.

5. Sebastian Edwards, "The Relationship between Exchange Rates and Inflation Targeting Revisited," NBER Working Paper 12163 (Cambridge, MA: National Bureau of Economic Research, 2006), 28–29.

monetization, especially in the Baltic states, Bulgaria, and Romania, while the Czech Republic, Slovakia, and Poland managed to avoid such credit increases (figure 2.8).[6] Credit booms are the harbingers of economic booms, but they lead to busts when long-term capital movements (foreign direct investment) are overtaken by short-term speculative capital flows (bank loans). Correspondingly, the four countries in the region with fixed exchange rates had the highest inflation in 2008 (figure 2.9). Clearly, a pegged exchange rate attracted more short-term capital, which was monetized and boosted inflation, but Romania with its floating exchange rate suffered as well. In Central Europe investment conditions and growth prospects were less attractive, as much of the economic convergence with the old EU countries had already taken place, which restrained capital inflows.

The countries with floating exchange rates had remarkably poorer fiscal discipline and lower growth than the currency board countries. The four floaters had on average budget deficits that exceeded those of countries with currency boards by no less than 4.7 percent of GDP from 2002 to 2007 (figure 2.10). Because of the stringent budget rules of a currency board regime the four currency board countries had minimal public debt of only 13 percent of GDP in 2007 (figure 4.1). These countries had an annual average growth rate that was 2.3 percentage points higher than that of the four floaters in 2000–08.

Today, it is ironic to read Jiri Jonas and Frederic Mishkin's words: "Undershoots of the inflation targets have resulted in serious economic downturns that have eroded support for the central bank in both the Czech Republic and Poland."[7] Who would advocate such a loose monetary policy today? The Czech and Polish central bankers successfully contained asset bubbles.

The Baltic Exchange Rate Conundrum

The exchange rate dilemma was particularly difficult for the three Baltic states. When these countries entered the European Union in May 2004, they received huge, unanticipated capital inflows, which they could not stop as they had relinquished capital controls in line with EU requirements and maintained a fixed exchange rate because of their currency boards. All three wanted to adopt the euro as soon as possible, as their national currencies were already tied to the euro, and they were small

---

6. Pradeep Mitra, Marcelo Selowsky, and Juan Zalduendo, *Turmoil at Twenty: Recession, Recovery, and Reform in Central and Eastern Europe and the Former Soviet Union* (Washington: World Bank, 2009), 5.

7. Jiri Jonas and Frederic S. Mishkin, "Inflation Targeting in Transition Economies: Experience and Prospects," in *The Inflation Targeting Debate*, eds. Ben S. Bernanke and Michael Woodford (Chicago: University of Chicago Press for the National Bureau of Economic Research, 2005), 409.

Figure 4.1 Public debt as share of GDP, 2000–09e

percent of GDP

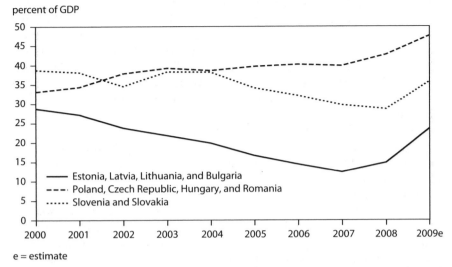

e = estimate

Sources: European Bank for Reconstruction and Development, *Transition Reports,* 2006, 2007, 2008, and 2009; IMF Country Reports, www.imf.org (accessed on April 12, 2010); Eurostat database, http://epp.eurostat.ec.europa.eu (accessed on May 4, 2010); author's calculations.

open economies with most trade in euros. Estonia and Lithuania joined the ERM II immediately in 2004 and Latvia did so in 2005.

The Baltic countries presumed that they would be able to adopt the euro within two to three years. The ECB and the European Commission accepted their fixed peg, but on the condition that the Balts give up the standard ECB commitment to supply automatic and unlimited foreign exchange intervention and financing whenever an exchange rate in ERM II reached its fluctuation margins. At the time, nobody thought much about this, since the Baltic economies were Europe's star performers, expecting no need for emergency funding, but in 2008 that turned out to be important.

Lithuania had planned to adopt the euro on January 1, 2007. In March 2006, it requested to be admitted into the EMU, but in its Convergence Report, the European Commission concluded: "Lithuania has made significant progress towards reaching a high degree of sustainable convergence by meeting the criteria on public finances, exchange rate stability and long-term interest rates. Lithuania does not, as yet, meet the criterion on price stability."[8]

Assessing Lithuanian 12-month average inflation, the Commission

---

8. European Commission, "2006 Convergence Report on Lithuania," *European Economy,* Special Report no. 2 (Brussels, 2006), 12.

observed in May 2006: "In March 2006 the reference value was 2.6 percent, calculated as the average of the 12-month average inflation rates in the three best-performing Member States (Sweden, Finland, and Poland) plus 1.5 percentage points. The corresponding inflation rate in Lithuania was 2.7 percent, 0.1 percentage points above the reference value."[9] No complaint could be smaller, and no judgment harsher. This was a preliminary number well within the statistical margin of error, but the European Commission exploited this minute distinction to pass its seemingly political verdict without any further explanation. Moreover, Poland and Sweden did not even belong to the EMU. That year, EMU members Portugal, Greece, and Italy exceeded the Maastricht budget ceiling of 3 percent of GDP as usual, as did Germany from 2002 to 2005 and France from 2002 to 2004.

The European Council accepted the recommendation from the Commission in its decision, as it usually does. If the European Commission had allowed Lithuania to adopt the euro like Slovenia in January 2007, it could have mitigated the current crisis. It is difficult to make sense of its decision, which benefited nobody.

Estonia and Latvia had already slightly higher inflation, and as it caught on, the euro adoption strategy of the three Baltic countries was blocked. Rather than contemplating an alternative strategy, they were dizzy with economic success. The weak coalition governments in Latvia and Lithuania could hardly hit the brakes, and their means were limited to discretionary fiscal policy and prudential bank regulation. The IMF warned repeatedly about the overheating in the Baltics and elsewhere in Eastern and Southern Europe as did independent economists, but to little avail: "By conventional standards, the external imbalances of many of the Central and Eastern European countries are large enough to justify serious concern" and they "stand out for having relatively small official reserves compared to their short-term external debt."[10] Few listened in the midst of a tremendous boom, and many countries managed large current account deficits for many years.

The Baltic countries could have pursued stricter bank regulation, but almost the whole world was failing in this regard. Most banks in Eastern Europe were big West European banks, and the East European bank regulators were too weak and respectful to question these presumed masters. Moreover, if domestic regulation had been too restrictive, domestic borrowers could easily have borrowed directly outside the country. The

9. Ibid., 26.

10. Susan Schadler, "Are Large External Imbalances in Central Europe Sustainable?" in *Challenges of Globalization: Imbalances and Growth*, eds. Anders Åslund and Marek Dabrowski (Washington: Peterson Institute for International Economics, 2008), 38; Philip R. Lane and Gian Maria Milesi-Ferretti, "Capital Flows to Central and Eastern Europe," *Emerging Markets Review* 8, no. 2 (2007): 106–23.

European Union had no inter-European bank regulation, a gap that is now about to be filled. To the national financial regulators, notably in Austria and Sweden, monetary expansion in the east was of little concern and they did not see it as their issue. Bank regulation was set in a competition toward the loosest possible standards. Yet Latvia started tightening bank regulation in 2007.

Fiscal policy remained prudent. Until 2008, Latvia and Lithuania had almost balanced budgets, while Estonia and Bulgaria were fiscally very conservative with budget surpluses of 2 to 3 percent of GDP in 2006 and 2007. Consequently, they had hardly any public debt, and Estonia even accumulated a reserve fund from its budget surpluses.

The Baltic countries also suffered from huge structural distortions, as finance and construction crowded out manufacturing. In 2008, the financial sector in Estonia and Latvia accounted for no less than 24 percent of GDP—twice as much as in the United States during the height of the bubble. The construction sectors were also large, contributing 8 to 10 percent of GDP.[11]

In effect, their EU entry put the Baltic states in an untenable situation. Their decade-old currency boards had won public acclaim, and it was politically impossible to abandon them. Yet, their EU entry led to excessive capital inflow, and the European Union prohibited capital controls, rendering control of inflation impossible, but because of their high inflation they were not allowed to adopt the euro. The European Union and the ECB offered no solution.

In hindsight, it is easy to argue that the Baltic states should have abandoned their currency boards with fixed exchange rates in 2004 to preempt overheating, but that was not obvious at the time and it would have been politically impossible. The populations embraced their stable exchange rates, which had saved them from the ravages of post-Soviet collapse. Ben Slay and Michaela Pospíšilová have convincingly argued that "there is little that the Baltic policy makers could/should have done differently."[12]

Yet the judgment is not clear cut. The currency board countries have maintained the best fiscal discipline and the highest economic growth while proving more vulnerable to capital inflows. Exchange rate flexibility eases adjustments and makes it easier to control inflation and thus avoid overheating, but currency boards provide better fiscal discipline than other monetary regimes and promote more structural reform.

11. Bas B. Bakker and Anne-Marie Gulde, "The Credit Boom in the EU New Member States: Bad Luck or Bad Policies?" IMF Working Paper 10/130 (Washington: International Monetary Fund, 2010), 24.

12. Ben Slay and Michaela Pospíšilová, "The Baltic Conundrum," CASE Network E-briefs 9/2009 (Warsaw: Centre for Social and Economic Research, August 2009), www.case-research.eu.

Why Latvia Did Not Have to Devalue Like Argentina

The Latvian crisis attracted the greatest international attention. From the outset, many prominent American economists—such as Paul Krugman, Nouriel Roubini, and Kenneth Rogoff—insisted that "Latvia is the new Argentina," to quote Nobel Prize winner Krugman. Their contention was that it was only a matter of time before Latvia was forced to devalue its currency and that no other way out of the crisis existed.[13] But no devaluation took place and the Latvian economy is safely returning to growth after two and a half years of negative growth, showing that no devaluation is necessary. This is an opportune moment to analyze an evidently flawed argument.[14]

The similarities between the Argentine and Latvian crises are rather limited. Nor do they suggest that Latvia should emulate Argentina's spectacular failure. Both countries had fixed exchange rates and incomplete currency boards, which led to the overvaluation of their exchange rates because of excessive inflation and large current account deficits. They required large IMF programs. But the parallels stop there. Rather than following Argentina into the abyss of failure, Latvia could use Argentina as an example of what not to do.

Argentina's failure was not a given. In his excellent book, *Argentina and the Fund: From Triumph to Tragedy*, Michael Mussa points out that "the tragedy in Argentina is epic not because, as in most tragedies, it was inevitable, but because it was avoidable."[15] Argentina's economy performed very well in the 1990s. Mussa argues that as late as mid-2001, the collapse could have been avoided, if sufficient measures had been taken.[16] He proceeds, "the fundamental cause of Argentina's tragedy was not primarily the Convertibility Plan [currency board]. Rather, it was the large and persistent excess of public spending over recurring revenues that led to an unsustainable accumulation of public debt and ultimately to sovereign default...."[17]

---

13. Paul Krugman, "Latvia is the New Argentina," New York Times blog, December 23, 2008, available at http://krugman.blogs.nytimes.com; Nouriel Roubini, "Latvia's Currency Crisis Is a Rerun of Argentina's," *Financial Times*, June 11, 2009; Edward Hugh, "Why the IMF's Decision to Agree to a Latvian Bailout Programme Without Devaluation Is a Mistake," *RGE Monitor*, December 22, 2008; Niklas Magnusson, "Rogoff Says Latvia Should Devalue Its Currency," Bloomberg News, June 29, 2009.

14. I laid out my contrarian arguments in December 2008: Anders Åslund, "Why Latvia Should Not Devalue," Realtime Economic Issues Watch, Peterson Institute for International Economics, December 9, 2008, www.piie.com.

15. Michael Mussa, *Argentina and the Fund: From Triumph to Tragedy* (Washington: Institute for International Economics, 2002), 51.

16. Ibid., 24.

17. Ibid., 51.

Nor was devaluation good for Argentina, but a costly failure. In the 1990s, Argentina had developed a sound banking system with substantial participation of foreign banks, which the default and devaluation demolished. When the peso plummeted, the banks suffered large currency losses because of their peso assets and dollar liabilities. The government aggravated their hammering by mandating that dollar loans of Argentine banks be paid in pesos, while converting dollar deposits into pesos at an unfavorable exchange rate.[18] Why would anybody want to repeat such an awful experience?

The only argument for an early devaluation was that it would become necessary in any case, and meanwhile Latvia's debt would rise and aggravate the crisis. As Nouriel Roubini put it in June 2009: "...devaluation seems unavoidable and the IMF program—which ruled it out—is thus inherently flawed."[19] Edward Hugh, a persistent advocate of devaluation, argued: "I am almost certain that the attempt to sustain [the peg] will fail (and that we will see some kind of rerun of Argentina 2000—in all the three Baltic countries and Bulgaria)."[20] Moreover, IMF credits, unlike debt to private lenders, cannot be written off. The conclusion is not that a stabilization program should not be tried but that it had to be sufficiently rigorous to succeed and the government strong enough to carry out the necessary fiscal cuts and structural reforms. Argentina lacked these abilities, but that was no reason for Latvia to fail.

The origin of the Latvian financial crisis lay in the overvaluation of the lat, which had led to a huge current account deficit and the accumulation of excessive private debt. The conventional wisdom claimed that such large foreign imbalances could be corrected only through depreciation, as in Thailand, Indonesia, Malaysia, and South Korea in 1997–98, in Russia in 1998, and in Argentina in 2001. Also the ERM, with European countries being pegged to the deutsche mark, fell apart with the devaluations of Sweden, Britain, and Italy in 1992. But this is a selective reading of monetary history. Multiple exchange rate regimes persist in the world, and most currencies—especially of small countries—are pegged to other currencies. The conventional wisdom of ideal exchange rate policy keeps changing.

Stanford economists Peter Blair Henry and Conrad Miller have argued that Barbados has been economically more successful than Jamaica because Barbados pegged its exchange rate to the US dollar in 1975 and has successfully maintained it for 35 years. In 1991, Barbados experienced a serious current account crisis and "the IMF recommended devaluation," but "the Barbadians resisted the recommendation." "Instead of devaluing,

---

18. Ibid., 62–63, 73.

19. Roubini, "Latvia's Currency Crisis Is a Rerun of Argentina's."

20. Hugh, "Why the IMF's Decision to Agree to a Latvian Bailout Programme Without Devaluation Is a Mistake."

the government began a set of negotiations with employers, unions, and workers that culminated with a tripartite protocol on wages and prices in 1993," in which "workers and unions assented to a one-time cut in real wages of about 9 percent.... The fall in real wages helped restore external competitiveness and profitability.... The economy recovered quickly."[21] Unlike Barbados, Jamaica devalued repeatedly, which made it possible to keep costs under control without structural reforms. Little wonder that the Barbados economy has been so much more successful.

In 1982, Denmark pegged its krone to the deutsche mark, which still holds after 28 years. It forced Denmark to tighten its fiscal policy and helped it launch radical liberalizing reforms a decade before Sweden and Finland, which continued to devalue rather than reform.[22] As a consequence, Denmark has surpassed Sweden in economic growth.

Empirically, devaluation is not inevitable in a severe current account crisis. Devaluation brings fast cost relief, but many countries have ended up in a vicious inflation-and-devaluation circle. The maintenance of a peg compels a country to undertake vital structural reforms to improve the functioning of its market. Therefore a peg may offer a safer exit out of a crisis. Barbados, Denmark, and many other countries have shown that a peg can enforce economic discipline and facilitate structural reforms.

Roubini lamented about Latvia: "Draconian cuts in public spending will be required if Latvia is to improve the current account. But this is becoming politically unsustainable. And while fiscal consolidation is needed…it will make the recession more severe in the short run. So it is a self-defeating strategy as long as the currency remains overvalued."[23] But Latvia had already shown that its draconian cuts were politically sustainable. Devaluation was never a serious option for the Latvian government and never enjoyed popular support, as was the case in Estonia, Lithuania, and Bulgaria, the other three countries with currency boards.

Latvia's budget deficit was entirely caused by the crisis, and its government was determined to fix the situation. Many economists make Roubini's mistake to assume that draconian cuts are impossible, but they are common. Most post-Soviet countries have cut public expenditures by 8 to 10 percent of GDP in crises (for example, Russia and Moldova in 1998–99). It is usually easier to cut public expenditures by 10 percent of GDP than 2 percent of GDP, because people realize that the crisis is real and has to be resolved. The Latvians are committed to their economic

21. Peter Blair Henry and Conrad Miller, "Institutions versus Policies: A Tale of Two Islands," *American Economic Review* 99, no. 2 (2009): 261–67.

22. Peter Erling Nielsen, "Dansk pengepolitik under forvandling [Danish Monetary Policy in Transformation]," *Nationaløkonomisk Tidsskrift* 124 (1986): 40–50. I owe this reference to Jacob Kirkegaard.

23. Roubini, "Latvia's Currency Crisis Is a Rerun of Argentina's."

success. After eight years of an average GDP growth of 9 percent, they were prepared to endure quite a bit of suffering.

The goal of any government under current account distress is to reduce costs, and the ideal way is to cut them directly: salaries, prices, and public expenditures. Unit labor costs are best reduced through systemic reforms. Devaluation is only a second-best solution if the government lacks the political strength to undertake direct cuts, because it boosts the foreign debt burden, eases the need for structural reform, and endangers the banking system of the crisis country. By standing firm, the Baltic governments forced necessary structural reforms on their post-Soviet public sector, which had too large an administration, far too many teachers and hospital beds, and underutilized real estate.

There are also structural differences. As the *Financial Times* observed: "...in small countries such as Latvia, unlike Argentina, relatively limited multilateral aid can go a long way."[24] Latvia is a very open economy, but Argentina is rather closed. Thanks to cost cuts and reduced demand for imports, the current account turned positive as early as January 2009, and prices are falling. Latvia turned around a current account deficit of 23 percent of GDP in 2007 to a stunning current account surplus of 9.4 percent of GDP in 2009.[25] Since July 2009, the Bank of Latvia has had little need to intervene on the currency market to defend the lat. In the first quarter of 2010, Latvia's exports rose by 10 percent in annualized terms.

The recession was certainly severe, but would it have been better if Latvia devalued? Rogoff argued: "The IMF made the wrong decision when it allowed Latvia to keep its currency peg.... In a normal situation, Latvia would already have devalued the lats and defaulted on its debt."[26] Why put Latvia in default and blow up its banking system when it had already proven unnecessary? By contrast, opposing devaluation, Mary Stokes reckoned: "The departure of these banks from the Baltics would be a massive blow to financial stability and consequently, it would impede economic recovery in the Baltics...."[27] As an EU member, Latvia benefited from ample financial support, while Argentina was on its own. Moreover, Latvia has a natural exit from its euro peg, namely the adoption of the euro, while Argentina had no such way out.

Rogoff noted: "If Latvia devalued, there is a risk that the turbulence would spread to other countries, which is why the IMF is supporting Latvia."[28] Indeed, Christoph Rosenberg mentioned as an important reason

24. "Riga Mortis," *Financial Times*, May 14, 2009.

25. International Monetary Fund, *World Economic Outlook* (Washington, April 2010), 54.

26. Magnusson, "Rogoff Says Latvia Should Devalue Its Currency."

27. Mary Stokes, "Devaluation in Latvia: Why Not?" *RGE Monitor*, December 31, 2008.

28. Magnusson, "Rogoff Says Latvia Should Devalue Its Currency."

for the IMF program with Latvia that "a devaluation in Latvia would have severe regional contagion effects."[29] Until June 2009, fears were great that a Latvian devaluation would have forced Lithuania, Estonia, and possibly Bulgaria to devalue. The freely floating currencies in the neighborhood— the Polish zloty, the Swedish krona, the Czech krona, and the Hungarian forint—could have taken a beating of 15 to 20 percent again. Moreover, since the IMF provided less than one-quarter of the financing, this was not really an IMF program but an IMF-EU-Nordic program, and the IMF had to listen to the cofinanciers, who all insisted on the maintenance of Latvia's peg.[30]

An important economic difference is that Latvia has a tradition of fiscal conservatism, having been persistently close to budget balance with minimal public debt. Argentina had a lasting large budget deficit and accumulated substantial public debt of about 50 percent of GDP,[31] while Latvia's was 9 percent of GDP at the end of 2007.[32] Argentina had a long record of high inflation, failed reforms, and stabilization programs and a large number of external defaults. Latvia, by contrast, has been a successful reformer.

It was easy to speculate against Argentina's deep and liquid debt market. By "late 2000, the Argentine government was the largest emerging market borrower on international credit markets, with outstanding obligations amounting to slightly more than 20 percent of the entire asset class."[33] But it is very difficult to speculate against the lat because the Latvian economy is so small, its financial sector tiny, and lats are rarely used. Liquidity is minimal. Few financial assets denominated in lat can be sold short. Of all loans in the Latvian economy, 87 percent are made in euros. In July 2009, Latvia's international reserves were about $5.5 billion, almost equaling both the $1.65 billion of lats in circulation and total bank deposits in lats of $4.2 billion.[34] Total outstanding government bonds in lats were only $1.9 billion, and the stock market was minuscule. A senior investment banker told me that their customers only speculated through credit default swaps to avoid counterparty risk. Even so the credit default swap rate fell from a high of 1,100 basis points in March 2009 to a moderate level of 400 basis points by late September, compared

29. Christoph Rosenberg, "Why the IMF Supports the Latvian Currency Peg," *RGE Monitor*, January 6, 2009; Stokes, "Devaluation in Latvia."

30. Rosenberg, "Why the IMF Supports the Latvian Currency Peg."

31. Mussa, *Argentina and the Fund*, 34.

32. European Bank for Reconstruction and Development, www.ebrd.com (accessed on April 12, 2010).

33. Mussa, *Argentina and the Fund*, 27.

34. Information from the Bank of Latvia website, www.bank.lv.

with 5,000 basis points for Ukraine in February 2009 (which did not result in default either).

The only similarities between Latvia and Argentina are that they had fixed exchange rates, ended up in severe financial difficulties, and required IMF programs. Striking any analogy between them would be surprising; solutions to their difficulties should be different.[35]

Multiple Exchange Rate Options Remain

The thinking about exchange rate regimes continues to evolve. In the 1990s, after the collapse of the European Monetary System in 1992, the East Asian crisis of 1997–98, and the Russian financial crisis of 1998, the conventional wisdom was that pegs were harmful.

The success of the currency boards in the Baltics and Bulgaria in the 1990s in parallel with the successful proliferation of inflation targeting from New Zealand in 1990 bred the view that the exchange rate should be either firmly fixed or floating. Currency boards were perceived as suitable for small, diversified, open economies, dominated by trade in one currency, especially after extreme macroeconomic instability, thus fitting the Baltics and Bulgaria perfectly.[36] However, one recent IMF study has found that intermediate exchange rate regimes have generated the best growth performance.[37] Slovakia is the only poignant example in my sample. But exchange rate regimes are often altered because of a crisis.

Another empirical IMF paper shows that exchange rate flexibility helped buffer the impact of the crisis.[38] Bas Bakker and Anne-Marie Gulde summarize convincingly: "Floating exchange rate had a much less pronounced credit boom, lower inflation, and smaller current account deficit.... They also had less deterioration of competitiveness, as they managed to prevent the acceleration of wages and prices that occurred in fixed exchange rate countries."[39] The literature on inflation targeting insists on many prerequisites for successful inflation targeting, but in the

35. Anders Åslund, "Why Latvia Should Not Devalue," Realtime Economic Issues Watch, Peterson Institute for International Economics, December 9, 2008, www.piie.com; Rosenberg, "Why the IMF Supports the Latvian Currency Peg."

36. John Williamson, *What Role for Currency Boards?* (Washington: Institute for International Economics, 1995).

37. Atish R. Ghosh, Jonathan D. Ostry, and Charamlambos Tsangarides, "Exchange Rate Regimes and the Stability of the International Monetary System," IMF Occasional Paper no. 270 (Washington: International Monetary Fund, 2010).

38. Pelin Berkmen, Gaston Gelos, Robert Rennhack, and James Walsh, "The Global Financial Crisis: Explaining Cross-Country Differences in the Output Impact," IMF Working Paper 09/280 (Washington: International Monetary Fund, 2009).

39. Bakker and Gulde, "The Credit Boom in the EU New Member States," 34.

transition countries it has been successful without these preconditions.[40] However, floating exchange rates plummeted during the crisis and brought about a real threat of banking and corporate debt crisis.

The currency boards have remained greatly popular in the four countries concerned. Their populations might have feared that devaluation would reduce their standard of living.[41] In Latvia, hardly anyone except a few oligarchs campaigned for devaluation. These wealthy exporters had the most to gain from devaluation, which naturally involves a regressive redistribution of income in favor of the wealthy.

The exchange rate conundrum remains unresolved, and none of the three main exchange rate regimes—fixed rates with currency board, temporary peg, or floating rate with inflation targeting—is altogether disqualified. Each has specific advantages and drawbacks. Currency boards are better at maintaining fiscal discipline, and inflation targeting is more effective at controlling the threat of excessive capital inflows. Yet, the credit boom and its bust were largely beyond national control.

The broader point is that no small open market economy can defend itself against loose monetary policy of the great monetary powers, the US Federal Reserve and the ECB. No exchange rate policy can resolve their dilemma. Very strict bank regulation in one small open economy is hardly possible, because banks will simply move abroad. Moreover, few governments can persuade voters to accept more than a couple percent of GDP in budget surplus. The best option for the small East European countries seems to be to join the ECB and insist on stricter monetary policy so they don't end up as the PIGS (Portugal, Italy, Greece, and Spain) in the future.

---

40. Jeffrey D. Amato and Stefan Gerlach, "Inflation Targeting in Emerging Market and Transition Economies: Lessons after a Decade," Discussion Paper no. 3074 (London: Center for Economic Policy Research, 2001).

41. Guillermo A. Calvo and Carmen M. Reinhart, "Fear of Floating," *Quarterly Journal of Economics 107*, no. 2 (2002): 379–408.

5

The Banking Crisis that Never Materialized

We must, indeed, all hang together, or assuredly we shall all hang separately.

—Benjamin Franklin, 1776

A peculiarity of the East European financial crisis was the large role played by West European banks. By 2008, their share of the banking sector in every single CEE-10 country exceeded two-thirds of the banking assets. No other sector was so dominated by foreign direct investment.

There were good economic reasons for this development. Successful East European bankers wanted to sell. Banks require a lot of capital, which is scarce in transition. Local businessmen who had developed banks reckoned that they could reap higher returns on their risk capital in other industries after the first wave of hyperprofits in the banking system. In addition, banking is a complex industry that requires plenty of skills and specialized human capital, which was in short supply in the postcommunist transition economies. Therefore all but a few local businessmen wanted to sell their banks when they had reached a certain size.

Luckily for the East European bank owners, many West European banks wanted to buy because they faced the opposite dilemma: They had a lot of capital and excellent staff at home but poor growth and returns. Their choice was to expand abroad or stagnate. Many opted for more profitable virgin markets in the east. They had all the resources to clean up rudimentary new eastern banks, and daring West European banks went on buying sprees in the east. They exported their capital and trained and managed personnel.

West European Banks Expand in the East

A group of 15 West European banks from seven countries—Austria, Belgium, France, Germany, Greece, Italy, and Sweden—dominated this eastern expansion. Most spectacular was Austrian Raiffeisen International Bank, which had been built by the colorful entrepreneur Herbert Stepic. It was based in Austria but was a purely East European bank with subsidiaries in 15 countries. Other Austrian banks, Bank Austria and Erste, responded to this competition. Another prominent bank in the east was Italian Unicredit. In the Baltic states, three Swedish banks—Swedbank, SEB, and Nordea—became dominant. The only non-European bank of significance in the region was American Citibank.

This looked like a coup for the European banks, and with banks came plenty of other business, allowing the European Union to completely dominate trade with Eastern Europe. The qualitative improvements of the East European banks were spectacular. Suddenly, the banking sector became the most modern and well-functioning sector of the East European economy, spearheading economic growth with a great credit boom.

Initially, most East European countries had been reluctant to allow foreigners to buy their banks. Usually, foreign investors were accepted only when banks had failed or after a financial crisis, for example, in the Baltics and the Balkans after the Russian financial crash of 1998. The foreign investors preferred to buy large banks with significant market power. Olena Havrylchyk and Emilia Jurzyk have identified no fewer than 77 such bank purchases in the eastern EU region. On average, acquired banks were less profitable but better capitalized than institutions that remained domestically owned.[1] Over time, however, foreign banks became more profitable.[2]

This development is easy to explain. To begin with, western banks bid up the prices of East European banks to sometimes five times the book value, when two times would have been normal. The seller, knowing the buyer's preference for large banks, tended to blow up the balance sheet with dubious loans before a sale thus profiting from asymmetric information, as the seller knew more than the buyer. After the sale, however, western banks could benefit from cheaper financing through the large-scale carry trade from Western to Eastern Europe. The West European banks contributed to the credit expansion becoming excessive, as they borrowed money cheaply at home and lent it to their new eastern subsidiaries, which lent to local customers, both companies and individuals, at a massive return. These borrowers did not mind high nominal interest rates, because inflation was rising and several countries with floating

---

1. Olena Havrylchyk and Emilia Jurzyk, "Inherited or Earned? Performance of Foreign Banks in Central and Eastern Europe," IMF Working Paper 10/4 (Washington: International Monetary Fund, 2010).

2. John Bonin, Iftekhar Hasan, and Paul Wachtel, "Bank Performance, Efficiency and Ownership in Transition Countries," *Journal of Banking and Finance* 29, no. 1 (2005): 31–53; R. De Haas and I. van Lelyveld, "Foreign Banks and Credit Stability in Central and Eastern Europe: A Panel Data Analysis," *Journal of Banking and Finance* 30 (2006): 1927–52.

exchange rates (the Czech Republic, Poland, and Slovakia) experienced large nominal appreciations. All parties were profiting from rising inflation in the east, which seemed risk-free.

This financial environment was demoralizing for bank customers as well. With cheap credits and sharply rising real asset prices, all borrowing made sense but saving did not. Consequently, the locals reduced their saving. The banks did not finance themselves through deposits but through loans from the old, stagnant European Union. In sharp contrast, in Latin America loans were funded primarily through domestic deposits rather than through loans or capital transfers from foreign parent banks, which restrained the credit expansion and foreign debt, while reducing foreign currency risks.[3] The consequence was that commercial banks in Eastern Europe as well as their customers exposed themselves to massive currency risks because of currency mismatches.

When the crisis hit, everything changed. Because of the magnitude of the credit expansion, it did attract attention in 2006 and 2007. Late in 2007, foreign banks started tightening their credit to Kazakhstan, Latvia, and Estonia, the three eastern countries with most obviously overheating banking systems. Yet, this remained a sideshow until September 2008, when the shockwave after the Lehman Brothers bankruptcy froze liquidity throughout the world. The most exposed East European countries—Hungary, Ukraine, and Latvia—were cut off from international financial markets.

The key problem was domestically owned banks in Eastern Europe, which had no access to ECB financing when short-term credits in Swiss francs dried up. The outstanding example was Parex Bank, Latvia's second-biggest bank, which the Latvian government had to take over. The biggest local bank in Hungary, OTP, was another prominent casualty, although it survived.

In these two countries, much of the political dispute in crisis resolution circulated around these two leading banks. As late as June 2010, the former owners of Parex Bank managed to mobilize a near majority in parliament to oust Latvia's minister of economy to refinance the "bad" Parex Bank, while the government tried to sell off the good part of the bank at any price to avoid further political manipulation. Whenever the government was forced to take over a privately owned domestic bank, political lobbying became extreme.[4] Politically, foreign banks were easier to handle.

In January–February 2009, the main concern was that the currencies of Poland, the Czech Republic, Hungary, and Romania were falling so deeply

---

3. Jorge Ivan Canales-Kriljenko, Brahima Coulibaly, and Herman Kamil, "A Tale of Two Regions," *Finance & Development* (March 2010): 35–36.

4. The same was true of the many tours around Nadra Bank in Ukraine and the many big bank crashes in Russia in 1998.

that the currency mismatch of both domestically owned and foreign banks could have forced them into bankruptcy. Fortunately, these currencies started recovering before any significant bank collapse took place.

In March 2009, another worry took center stage, when the Bank for International Settlements (BIS) presented stunning statistics on the exposure of West European banks to Eastern Europe. A typical headline read: "Subprime Eastern Europe to Bankrupt Western European Banks."[5] In particular, Austrian banks had outstanding loans to Eastern Europe amounting to 70 percent of the Austrian GDP. The focus fell on two West European countries, Austria because of its overall exposure and Sweden for its concentrated credits to the Baltic states. The gross figures were stark. Eastern Europe had borrowed a total of more than $1.7 trillion abroad mainly from West European banks, and in 2009 they had to repay or roll over about $400 billion or one-third of the region's GDP. Figure 5.1 shows the exposure of banks in the European Union to the CEE-10.[6]

These statistics were more scary than real. First, they included all East European countries, but Poland, the Czech Republic, Slovakia, and Slovenia were already in good shape. Second, a large share of these loans pertained to these banks' own subsidiaries in Eastern Europe, allowing them to control the risk. Third, thanks to globalization, not only these banks but the entire economies were so interlinked. After half a year of liquidity freeze, the vast majority of these loans was rolled over or refinanced.

Yet, the West European banks experienced a prisoner's dilemma, which was a real collective action problem. They knew that if all quit, each bank had better exit first, but it would be best for all of them if almost all stayed because then the East European banking system would not collapse because of capital flight. Benjamin Franklin's old saying from the signing of the Declaration of Independence applied: "We must, indeed, all hang together, or assuredly we shall all hang separately." The banks could hardly resolve this dilemma on their own, as they were more inclined to compete than to collude.

The main worry was not the behavior of the banks themselves but that the West European banks that were bailed out by their governments would be forced to sell their foreign subsidiaries as a condition of state aid. German Finance Minister Peer Steinbrück was reported to have flatly rejected the usage of any EU rescue funds for the east, claiming that it was not Germany's problem.[7]

---

5. "Subprime Eastern Europe to Bankrupt Western European Banks," *Market Oracle*, March 5, 2009, www.dailymarkets.com.

6. A characteristic scary article is by F. William Engdahl, "Next Wave of Banking Crisis to Come from Eastern Europe," GlobalResearch.ca, Centre for Research on Globalization, February 18, 2009.

7. Ibid.

Figure 5.1   Exposure of West European banks in CEE-10

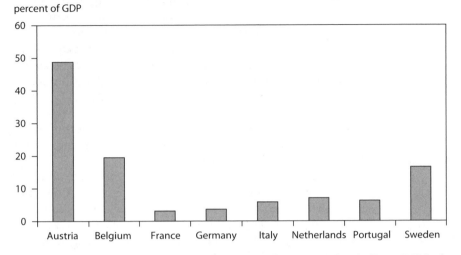

percent of GDP

Austria | Belgium | France | Germany | Italy | Netherlands | Portugal | Sweden

Sources: IMF, *World Economic Outlook,* April 2010, www.imf.org (accessed on April 28, 2010); Bank for International Settlements, Preliminary Report, April 22, 2010, table 9B, www.bis.org (accessed on April 28, 2010).

The Vienna Initiative

The European Bank for Reconstruction and Development (EBRD) and the International Monetary Fund (IMF) noticed this problem and brought together representatives of the World Bank, the European Investment Bank (EIB), and the European Commission as well as central banks, governments, and supervisory bodies to design a joint approach to tackle the banking crisis at a meeting at the Austrian Ministry of Finance in Vienna in January 2009. This informal process was called the European Bank Coordination Initiative and became known as the Vienna Initiative.[8] A forum for collective action to prevent a banking crisis had been established.

In the next step, substantial government money was mobilized for the recapitalization of the East European banking systems and was put forward in February 2009. In a Joint Action Plan, the EBRD, the EIB, and the World Bank committed themselves to provide €25 billion to banks in Eastern Europe and for lending to the real economy in 2009–10.

---

8. Both the EBRD and the IMF claim to have initiated this process, but the EBRD seems to claim more strongly. Thomas Mirow, "The Role of the EBRD in Overcoming the Financial Crisis in Central and Eastern Europe" (speech in Vienna, July 24, 2009); Camilla Andersen, "Agreement with Banks Limits Crisis in Emerging Europe," *IMF Survey Magazine,* October 28, 2009.

The third step was to make sure that West European banks were not forced by their governments to sell their eastern subsidiaries. In March 2009, the European Council held a summit and declared that domestic bank support packages should not be restricted to bank operations in their respective home markets. This was the critical breakthrough. Thanks to the abundant liquidity with which the ECB and other central banks had flooded the West European banks, they had plenty of cheap credit and many banks also recapitalized themselves through rights issues.

A fourth precondition for joint bank action was the adoption of an IMF standby program for each crisis country, which had already been concluded for several East European countries.

Finally, the EBRD and the IMF organized separate meetings with the main West European banks and persuaded them to agree on refinancing and recapitalization of the banking system for each country. Such programs were adopted for Bosnia, Hungary, Latvia, Romania, Serbia, and Ukraine.[9] For each crisis country only a subsection of banks actually present in that country were engaged. In parallel, the EBRD, EIB, and World Bank guaranteed financing for other weak or failed domestic banks as was necessary after their restructuring.

In comparison with Parex Bank and OTP, foreign banks have appeared timid in their lobbying. Naturally, the foreign banks, like most locals, have opposed devaluations, but they have had little influence on these decisions. All the currency board countries strongly opposed devaluation on their own. The foreign bankers' main interest was to facilitate foreclosure of properties but in this regard little has changed. Thus, foreign banks have been ineffective lobbyists.

Not a single CEE-10 country experienced problems with its payments system during the crisis, in sharp contrast to the Russian financial crash in, August 1998, when bank and credit card payments stalled for almost three months. Undoubtedly, many Western banks will alter strategy after the crisis is over, and bank mergers and consolidation should be forthcoming, but nobody wants to sell at firesale prices in the midst of a crisis if they are not forced to.

The outcome of this potential drama is impressive. No West European bank has withdrawn from any East European country. The most significant bank failure was Parex Bank in Latvia, but no serious banking crisis has erupted anywhere in the eastern European Union.[10] In fact, the banking structure in the whole region has been frozen. More creative destruction

---

9. European Commission, "European Bank Coordination Meeting: International Coordination Helped Avert a Systemic Bank Crisis in Central and Eastern Europe," press release, Brussels, September 25, 2009.

10. Even in Ukraine, where eight private domestic banks among the country's 30 biggest banks have collapsed, all 17 foreign banks maintained their subsidiaries.

and bank mergers could have been desirable, but the paramount objective was to salvage the banking system, and bank failures often proliferate.

As time passes, however, restructuring of the banking system becomes more necessary, while the risks decline. As of July 2010, virtually all banks are overwhelmingly cautious and barely give loans, since they are hoarding cash to cover their as yet unrevealed nonperforming loans. Nor have any new banks emerged as yet.

For the long term, the question remains, When is the best time to eliminate and merge banks to prepare the ground for new and better banks after the crisis, as happened in Eastern Europe after the Russian financial crash of 1998? Have policymakers been too afraid of a banking crisis for too long so as to avoid a new beginning?

6

International Cooperation in Crisis

> *...the question [is] whether it is better to be loved rather than feared, or feared rather than loved. It might perhaps be answered that we should wish to be both; but since love and fear can hardly exist together, if we must choose between them, it is far safer to be feared than loved....*

> —Niccolò Machiavelli

The East European financial crisis marks a considerable rebalancing of the roles of the main international players. The two winners were the International Monetary Fund (IMF) and the European Commission, while the losers were the United States and the World Bank. The European Central Bank (ECB) did not even enter the game.

International Monetary Fund: Financial Savior

In early 2008, the IMF suffered from its own financial crisis. Its problem was not lack of capital but a near absence of customers, and the Fund lived on the interest on its loans. Its loan portfolio had dwindled to less than $10 billion in April 2008, which left the IMF with an annual budget deficit of $400 million, pretty humiliating for the world's fiscal police.

In the spring of 2008, the new French Managing Director Dominique Strauss-Kahn reckoned that no financial crisis would occur any time soon so he laid off 600 professionals or about one-quarter of the Fund's professional staff to save money and satisfy its critics. One of them wrote: "The IMF's loss of influence is probably the most important change in the international financial system in more than half a century."[1] Little did he know what would happen within half a year.

By September, the financial warning bells were ringing shrill. A first new IMF standby credit was offered to Georgia in September 2008, but it

---

1. Mark Weisbrot, "The IMF's Dwindling Fortunes: Thanks to Disasters of Its Own Making, the Agency Is Losing Money and Influence," *Los Angeles Times*, April 27, 2008.

was caused by its war with Russia rather than the global financial crisis. The collapse of Lehman Brothers on September 15, 2008, led to rampant liquidity hoarding. By May 1, 2010, before the Greek stabilization program, the Fund had committed $170 billion for multiple new standby programs. The IMF was back in business and thrived.

The Fund had changed its policy considerably from the East Asian crisis in 1997–98. Then, it had demanded strict fiscal policy and far-reaching structural reforms at the height of the crisis to combat crony capitalism, which had attracted plenty of criticism for being onerous or even destabilizing. After talk in the late 1990s of a post–Washington Consensus with numerous structural conditions, the IMF went back to the original Washington Consensus, as formulated by John Williamson, with a few elementary conditions, essentially reasonable budget balance, tenable exchange rate policy, and decent reserve management.[2] The IMF largely ignored structural reforms, for which it has little competence. Instead, it paid more attention to bank restructuring. The essence of the IMF policy change was fewer conditions, the acceptance of much larger budget deficits than in the past, and much more financing than before. This was a sensible reaction to the greater financial globalization. It recognized that these financial problems involved liquidity rather than solidity, and the policy may be described as "back to basics."

The IMF has always been quick but it acted faster than ever, in both concluding standby agreements and disbursing money. A large number of IMF standby programs were swiftly adopted. In Eastern Europe, the IMF concluded programs for Hungary in October 2008, Ukraine in November, Latvia in December, Belarus and Serbia in January 2009, Armenia in March, Romania in May, Bosnia and Herzegovina in July, and Moldova in January 2010.

Initially the IMF demanded balanced budgets. As the crisis evolved, all growth forecasts and thus budget predictions deteriorated until the summer of 2009, and state revenues deteriorated with output. The IMF reacted by accepting ever larger budget deficits. Traditionally, it had financed international reserves of central banks, but now the IMF provided substantial budget funding that had usually been offered by the World Bank and bilateral donors. The IMF had outwitted and marginalized its Bretton Woods sister, the World Bank. Instead, it found a mighty new partner in the European Union.

The old ceilings on lending were abandoned. Previously, the IMF had limited its lending to the country's quota with the IMF for one year and three times the quota in total lending. Now, the IMF provided 12 times the quota in its two-year standby agreements and they were heavily front-

---

2. John Williamson, *Latin American Adjustment: How Much Has Happened?* (Washington: Institute for International Economics, 1990).

loaded, that is, the early tranches were larger than the later ones. The IMF instructions focused on financing need rather than formal limits.[3]

The most contentious issue was exchange rate policy. The IMF had a clear preference for inflation targeting with floating exchange rates. Since Hungary and Romania pursued inflation targeting, it had no quarrel with these two countries. The IMF demanded that Ukraine and Belarus let their exchange rates float and depreciate. Latvia's overvalued fixed exchange rate was a bone of contention.

The IMF made an embarrassing error in its important *Global Financial Stability Report* published in April 2009, where it presented the external debt refinancing needs for the East European countries as a ratio of their foreign exchange reserves. These data were roughly twice as high as the real ratios. After these numbers were questioned, the IMF corrected its mistakes, for example, cutting this ratio for the Czech Republic from 236 to 89 percent and Estonia's from 210 to 132 percent.[4] The IMF undermined confidence in crisis countries at a critical time through an elementary arithmetic mistake and lack of review of a key document, which was no small matter.

While the IMF's crisis resolution was impressive, its policy advice was not quite as stellar. In early 2008, the IMF, purportedly the high priest of fiscal orthodoxy, urged all who could to expand their borrowing and public spending, which included countries like Spain.[5]

Overall, the crisis was just what the IMF needed to revive itself. It gathered more financial resources, political standing, and power than it had ever had.

European Union: The Rookie

The new partner and competitor of the IMF was the European Union. Before the crisis, it was discussed whether the IMF or the European Union should take the lead. When the crisis hit, the discussion was over because Hungary, Latvia, and Romania all went to the IMF.

Iceland set a precedent. As is usually the case, the Icelanders denied the financial crisis until it erupted in late September 2008. Iceland is a wealthy Nordic country but not a member of the European Union. The other Nordic countries (Denmark, Finland, Norway, and Sweden) felt special responsibility and were prepared to assist, but as strong supporters

---

3. IMF, "Staff Guidance Note on the Use of Fund Resources for Budget Support" (photocopy, Washington, March 23, 2010).

4. Stefan Wagstyl and Jan Cienski, "Red-Faced IMF Fixes East Europe Error," *Financial Times*, May 7, 2009.

5. Jan Cienski and Stefan Wagstyl, "Poland Says IMF Advice Helped to Cause Unsustainable Debts," *Financial Times*, March 10, 2010.

of multilateralism they insisted the Icelandic stabilization program be managed by the IMF. Eventually, the Icelanders conceded to going to the IMF, and a staff-level agreement was announced on October 24, 2008.[6] When the crisis hit Hungary and Latvia hard and fast in October they followed the precedence of Iceland and turned to the IMF, while the European Commission and European countries provided cofinancing. As these countries were members of the European Union, but not of the Economic and Monetary Union (EMU), the European Commission acknowledged responsibility, while the ECB ignored them.

During the balance-of-payments crises in Southern Europe in the early 1990s, the European Commission had established a significant balance-of-payments support facility of €12 billion, which could lend to EU members that are not part of the EMU. The European Council quickly doubled it to €25 billion on December 2, 2008, and again to €50 billion on May 18, 2009.[7] By the end of 2009, €14.6 billion had been committed to Hungary, Latvia, and Romania. Thus, the European Union, like the IMF, had plenty of funds that could be used for budget support. Donors other than the IMF, the European Union, and individual EU countries were neither needed nor desired.

In line with an old tradition, the European Union cofinanced IMF programs. The relationship between the European Commission and the IMF became surprisingly harmonious. The IMF took the lead and formulated the programs, while the European Union and key EU members shadowed the IMF negotiations and concluded EU programs with the countries in crisis. The European Union provided about as much financing as the IMF, while it tended to issue fewer but larger tranches. The European Union, however, reserved its right to second-guess the IMF. The IMF was made accountable to a strong partner with the same aim but with the right to protest. In addition, neighboring Nordic countries contributed substantial bilateral funds to Latvia.

The European Commission had developed a new important function with surprising ease, but it bore a grudge against the IMF for being the leader. It wanted to take the lead but lacked the necessary competence.

European Central Bank: Voldemort

Two parties were conspicuous by their apparent absence, the European Central Bank and the United States. Most striking is that the ECB under

---

6. IMF, "IMF Announces Staff Level Agreement with Iceland on $2.1 Billion Loan," press release no. 08/256, October 24, 2008.

7. European Commission, *Report from the Commission of the European Parliament and the Council on Borrowing and Lending Activities of the European Union in 2008* (Brussels, March 4, 2010), http://eur-lex.europa.eu (accessed on April 20, 2010).

the presidency of Frenchman Jean-Claude Trichet played no role in Eastern Europe outside the EMU. One minister in the region told me that the ECB was like Voldemort in *Harry Potter*: He was so feared that nobody dared to pronounce his name.

Before the crisis, the ECB offered nothing to the new EU members. Even though the currency board countries had tied their currencies to the euro, the ECB seemed to ignore East European monetary conditions altogether, neglecting the East European credit boom. The European Union and the ECB failed to impose the Maastricht criteria on the EMU member states, while the ECB was part of the 2006 EU decision to block Lithuania from entering the EMU because its inflation was 2.6 percent. If Lithuania had been accepted, the Baltic financial crisis could possibly have been contained. Similarly, some ECB board members made private statements that Estonia should not be allowed to enter the eurozone in January 2011, although it had complied with all criteria. One was quoted suggesting that new criteria, such as GDP per capita, ought to be added.[8] At best, the ECB appeared a disinterested bystander, but the ERM II conditions for EMU entry contributed to the financial crisis.

Yet, by being so unhelpful, the ECB rendered the Maastricht conditions more effective in non-EMU eastern EU members than in the EMU. It imposed truly hard budget constraints on the new EU members that were obliged to enter the EMU in an indeterminate future and thus had to obey the Maastricht criteria. Meanwhile, the ECB and the European Union could do nothing to discipline the members of the EMU.

As the credit crunch started in September 2008, the ECB provided one important service to Eastern Europe. It pumped credits into eurozone banks, attempting to compensate for the liquidity that had dried up. Since many banks had subsidiaries in Central and Eastern Europe, it indirectly benefited Eastern Europe.

The US Federal Reserve provided credit swaps to many emerging-market economies, including Brazil, Mexico, Singapore, and South Korea.[9] Olivier Jeanne has argued that the US Federal Reserve swap arrangement of $30 billion was critical for South Korea's stabilization, although the country entered the crisis with some $270 billion of foreign currency reserves.[10] But Central or East European countries received no swap lines. The ECB gave swap credits only to Denmark and Sweden. It offered Hungary and Poland repurchase agreements in October and November

8. Juhan Tere, "ECB's Jürgen Stark Expressed Doubt over Estonia's Preparedness to Adopt the Euro," *Baltic Course*, April 16, 2010. I owe this reference to Barry Wood.

9. Maurice Obstfeld, Jay C. Shambaugh, and Alan M. Taylor, "Financial Instability, Reserves, and Central Bank Swap Lines in the Panic of 2008," NBER Working Paper 14826 (Cambridge, MA: National Bureau of Economic Research, 2008).

10. Olivier Jeanne, "Dealing with Volatile Capital Flows," Policy Briefs in International Economics 10-18 (Washington: Peterson Institute for International Economics, July 2010), 1.

2008, respectively, but they required highly liquid euro assets, rendering them insignificant. Hungary drew on its credit line, exchanging euro assets of similar liquidity, in the hope that the market would be deceived into believing that this was real credit. Poland had no need for such illusions and preferred to turn to the IMF, being the first customer of a precautionary flexible credit line facility of $20.5 billion in May 2009,[11] which was similar to a swap credit. Ironically, if Poland had not joined the European Union, the US Federal Reserve might very well have offered it a swap line. As Jeanne notes, "the US Federal Reserve provided liquidity more expeditiously than the IMF, with little conditionality or stigma effect."[12] But the IMF was more expeditious than the ECB for Eastern Europe's EU members.

Public ECB statements about Eastern Europe are few, but the ECB policy was clear. In January 2009, at the height of the liquidity squeeze, Yves Mersch, the governor of Luxembourg's central bank and an ECB governor, told the *Financial Times* that the ECB did not have "a mandate to be a regional United Nations agency."[13] Well, it was an EU agency owned by all the EU member states, not only by the members of the EMU. The ECB disregard for financial stability in the EU countries outside of the EMU is difficult to understand. It did nothing to mitigate the wild exchange rate moves in the fall of 2008 and early 2009 between the euro and EU countries with freely floating exchange rates, although this endangered the banking system in the eurozone.

The ECB and EU policy may be described as soft budget constraints for euro insiders and hard budget constraints for outsiders. ECOFIN, the council of EU ministers of finance, lost significance, as euro ministers of finance always met before ECOFIN and made the real decisions. In effect, the ECB and euro ministers of finance had divided the European Union into first- and second-class citizens. Tellingly, when the IMF-EU crisis package was composed on May 2, 2010, nobody even suggested that non-eurozone EU countries should contribute, as they had been so excluded.

The best that can be said of the ECB in the crisis is that Eastern Europe benefited from not having to deal with it. Apart from its timely expansion of liquidity, little can be said to its defense. The ECB lies at the heart of the EU malfunction. It goes beyond the scope of this book to analyze why it performed so poorly, which should be a key topic of research. Did its great independence breed unaccountable behavior? Did it have the wrong mandate? Did the constitutional arrangement render its governance dysfunctional? Or was it a matter of incompetence?

---

11. IMF, "IMF Executive Board Approves $20.58 Billion Arrangement for Poland under the flexible credit line," press release no. 09/153, May 6, 2009.

12. Jeanne, "Dealing with Volatile Capital Flows," 3.

13. Ralph Atkins and Stefan Wagstyl, "ECB Set to Rebuff Non-Euro Nations," *Financial Times*, January 23, 2009.

The United States: Keeping a Low Profile

Another party that was conspicuously absent was the United States. In the East Asian and Russian financial crises of 1997–98, the US Treasury had been all over for good and bad. The US Treasury was ready to organize international financing, and it had a strong view of what had to be done under the forceful leadership of Lawrence Summers.

In 2008 and 2009, the US government kept a very low profile in Eastern Europe. Concrete business was dealt with at a low level, rarely higher than undersecretary of the Treasury, and the US administration limited itself to the principles of IMF financing, while the European Commission took an active part in the negotiations.

The George W. Bush administration came in with a clear world view: It wanted to leave the outside world alone. Initially, it saw excessive international activism as a flaw of the Clinton administration. When it changed its view, Iraq became the dominant US foreign policy concern, marginalizing all other issues. Throughout the Bush administration, the US Treasury had much less political prominence than in the 1990s. In the Barack Obama administration, it took months before any senior international Treasury posts were occupied.

Both the United States and the old core EU countries, notably France and Germany, thought that Europe should resolve its own problems. Europe had sufficient resources and wanted to keep the United States and others out. The East Europeans, however, had a more pro-American view and felt abandoned by the United States. Almost all of them, including Hungary, Latvia, and Romania, were strong US allies in the North Atlantic Treaty Organization, and members of the Alliance of the Willing. They had sent troops to both Iraq and Afghanistan, and they were hurt when the United States ignored them when they ended up in financial crisis. Since the United States was not prepared to offer balance-of-payments support, it had no voice. It had even refused to provide balance-of-payments support to the Baltics in 1992. US interference would only have restrained the generosity of others as in the former Soviet Union in the 1990s.[14]

The financial crisis had started in the United States, so American policymakers were overwhelmed by domestic work and kept a much lower international profile than before. Moreover, the global view of US economic insights was not very favorable, so few solicited American government views.

Yet, it can also be argued that the United States assisted more effectively by keeping a low profile. The key source of support was the IMF. In the 1990s, the United States had persistently argued for large financial aid

---

14. The United States did not contribute to the $1 billion stabilization program for the three Baltic states in 1992; see Anders Åslund, *Building Capitalism: The Transformation of the Former Soviet Bloc* (New York: Cambridge University Press, 2002), 404.

packages from the IMF, especially for Mexico in 1994, but the Europeans had said no. In September 2008, new ice was broken when the Europeans, in a reversal of roles, wanted to offer Iceland 12 times its IMF quota. The United States quietly agreed. As the Hungarian, Latvian, and Romanian programs came to the fore, packages around 12 times the quota became standard. Another advantage of the near silence of the US administration was that the US Congress was not awoken and raised no protests against these new large IMF aid packages—contrary to what had been the case in the 1990s. Without apparent US interest, but with US consent, the IMF could evolve in a more multilateral fashion, and the European Union was forced to take more responsibility.

The US policy is open to interpretation. Overtly, this crisis seems to have marked the beginning of the end of the United States as the dominant global power because it played no apparent role. Yet, an alternative interpretation is that the United States pursued successful quiet diplomacy. It got what it wanted—large IMF financing to European countries in crisis—without arousing either domestic or international opposition. In addition, no demands were raised about bilateral American financing, while the EU and European countries provided more financing than the IMF. The United States made sure that its allies in Eastern Europe were assisted, but those allies felt alienated.

In effect, the United States appears to have followed the policy advice of Edwin M. Truman:

> The major policy instrument available to the United States to contain the European crisis aftermath is the International Monetary Fund. The United States should continue to provide maximum, constructive support for the IMF in carrying out its responsibilities for the promotion of global growth and financial stability.[15]

World Bank: The Third Fiddle

Traditionally, the World Bank had played a major role in IMF-led stabilization efforts, but it typically played the second fiddle, much to its chagrin.[16] The new World Bank management under President Robert Zoellick wanted a different role for the Bank. It argued that Europe was no concern of the World Bank, which ought to focus on the developing world, where it greatly expanded its activities. In effect, it ceded the position of second fiddle to the European Bank for Reconstruction and Development.

---

15. Edwin M. Truman, "The Role of the International Monetary Fund and Federal Reserve in the Stabilization of Europe," testimony before the US House Committee on Financial Services, Subcommittee on International Monetary Policy and Subcommittee on Domestic Monetary Policy and Technology, May 20, 2010.

16. Sebastian Mallaby, *The World's Banker* (New York: Penguin Press, 2004).

The Bank did contribute small amounts to the East European IMF programs, focusing on the restructuring of the banking system, but it played a minor role in East European stabilization after the IMF, the European Commission, and the European Bank for Reconstruction and Development.

A New Pattern of International Financial Crisis Resolution

Overall, international cooperation in financial crisis resolution in Eastern Europe functioned well. When Hungary asked the IMF for financial assistance in October 2008, the IMF was more than happy to take the lead. The European Commission accepted ceding the leadership to the IMF because the IMF had all that was needed: experienced staff, contractual procedures, controls, and large financing. Instead, the Commission contributed with cofinancing of the IMF agreements, and it provided a valuable check. Hungary's request was followed by those of Latvia in December and Romania in March 2009.

A pattern quickly developed. The IMF negotiated the stabilization programs while the Commission cofinanced IMF standby programs for EU members but did nothing for non-EU countries (Ukraine, Moldova, and Belarus). In the case of Latvia, the European Union provided more financing than the IMF, and bilateral funding from individual European countries—the Nordic countries, Estonia, Poland, and the Czech Republic—played an important role.

The IMF outflanked the World Bank, which played a supportive role in bank restructuring, and the European Union acted when the United States stayed in the background. The big question is why the ECB was passive. Two other international financial institutions also played an important, supportive role in bank restructuring, namely the European Bank for Reconstruction and Development and the European Investment Bank, an EU institution.

7

Why Eastern Europe Acted So Responsibly

He who has clean hands and a pure heart, who has not lifted up
his soul to falsehood and has not sworn deceitfully.

—Psalm 24:4

Eastern Europe stands out for its virtuous fiscal and structural policies. At the end of 2008, the CEE-10 countries had an unweighted average public debt of 27 percent of GDP compared with 58 percent of GDP in the EU-15. These new EU members kept their public deficits small thanks to comparatively low public expenditures. Their taxes were generally moderate, especially corporate profit taxes, which were around 19 percent, and personal income taxes were mostly flat in the range of 10 to 23 percent.

After the crisis hit, virtually all countries in the region pursued a responsible economic policy. They had no room for additional fiscal stimulus but cut public expenditures and salaries as they found necessary. In spite of the crisis hitting Eastern Europe slightly more severely than Western Europe, thus undermining their state revenues more, the CEE-10 countries had an average budget deficit of 5.7 percent of GDP in 2009 compared with 6.5 percent in the wealthier EU-15.

Many observers worried that the crisis would provoke social unrest in the European transition countries, but it has been minimal. A few incidents occurred—minor riots in Riga on January 13, 2009 and similar protests in Vilnius the next day, but the unrest stopped there. Also, strikes and other social upheavals have been rare. The biggest might have occurred in Romania in May 2010 in a second round of cuts, involving public-sector wage and pension cuts.

Strong Center-Right Tendency in Elections

In early June 2009, all EU countries elected a new European Parliament. Participation in these not very important elections tends to be low, and protest votes for populist or extreme parties are common, but they reflect the political mood. The big winners in the 2009 European elections were the center-right parties, which stood for fiscal constraint and free markets. Together the center-right parties and the liberals won a substantial majority in every single CEE-10 country. The biggest winner in the region was Poland's ruling center-right party, Civic Platform. The hard right benefited in only two countries, the Jobbik party in Hungary (14.8 percent of the votes) and the Greater Romania Party in Romania (8.6 percent), which is not much in comparison with Jean-Marie Le Pen's National Front in France. The big losers were the remaining socialist parties, while the communist parties had already been eliminated. The voters clarified that they wanted stricter market economic policies, and the protest vote surprised with its near absence.

The democratic process in the CEE-10 has continued to function as before. No regime change has occurred, though several countries have changed governments, and they have done so in a normal democratic manner. Government changes have been frequent after the end of communism. Traditionally, the three Baltic states, Poland, and Bulgaria have altered government almost every year. The changes of government have not been dramatic, but their overall tendency is clearly center-right favoring more resolute crisis managers.

Elections in Eastern Europe focus on corruption, and voters rightly judge the incumbents as guilty, so the loss of the incumbent government is standard. But the financial crisis has been a major theme in recent national parliamentary elections. The political trend has been overwhelmingly toward the center-right parties, which have won in nearly all the CEE-10 countries. Eight changed government in the 22 months from September 2008, and in seven countries the same forces were victorious. As of August 2010, only one CEE-10 country, Slovenia, has a center-left government, while the nine others have center-right governments. The moderate right has grown stronger than ever because of the crisis and has won and advocated stricter fiscal policies, with Hungary being a possible exception where a right-wing populist party rules.

Lithuania. In October 2008, the socialist government lost parliamentary elections to a center-right coalition led by the Homeland Union party, whose leader Andrius Kubilius became prime minister.

Latvia. In February 2009, the rather oligarchic Latvian center-right government under Ivars Godmanis collapsed and was replaced with a more free-market center-right government under Valdis Dombrovskis, although its parliamentary base was similar.

Bulgaria. Ordinary parliamentary elections on July 5, 2009 led to the ouster of the center-left government by the new center-right party Citizens for European Development of Bulgaria, headed by Boyko Borisov, who became prime minister with a big majority.

Romania. Close presidential elections in November and December 2009 eventually led to the victory of the incumbent center-right President Traian Băsescu, and a renewed center-right government under Prime Minister Emil Boc tightened fiscal policies.

Hungary. The socialist government of Ferenc Gyurcsány fell at a party convention in March 2009 because of its prior fiscal irresponsibility and his statement that he had been systematically lying. His government was quickly replaced by another socialist government led by Gordon Bajnai, which carried out a radical fiscal restructuring. It was devastated in the parliamentary elections in April 2010 by Viktor Orbán's center-right Young Democrats party, which won on a populist platform and currently appears the least fiscally responsible government in the region.

Czech Republic. The center-right government of Mirek Topolanek fell in March 2009 in a vote of no confidence. His government was fatally wounded by a series of scandals rather than by any looming financial melt-down and also by personal opposition from fellow conservative President Václav Klaus. The outcome was a nonpolitical caretaker government, and economic policy did not change. In April 2010, three center-right parties— two of them new anticorruption parties—unexpectedly won a big victory.

Slovakia. A center-left populist three-party coalition government sat firmly until the parliamentary elections in June 2010, which were won by three center-right parties, contrary to expectations, just as in the Czech Republic.

Slovenia. The only exception to the center-right trend was Slovenia, which held parliamentary elections on September 21, 2008, just before the financial crisis broke. The social democrats became the biggest party, formed a new center-left coalition, and took over from the incumbent center-right coalition, while economic policy hardly changed.

Causes of Popular Fiscal Restraint

The CEE-10 countries were hit by tremendous shocks of GDP declines. Yet their populations did not protest but opted for more determined right-wing governments, which favored strict fiscal policies and market-oriented structural reforms in the midst of the crisis. This picture runs counter to much of the current academic writing on political economy along the ideas of "rational expectations" and "tradeoffs" between different social groups. Yet voters were not looking for their own marginal benefits but for a viable future of their nations.

Why did these nations behave so responsibly? Quite a few alternative explanations are possible. One can distinguish between at least four groups of explanations: excellent prior growth, concerns about national sovereignty, recent experiences of crises, and equitable reform programs.

All of Eastern Europe had enjoyed nearly a decade of high economic growth from 2000 to 2007. Many thought that they had just been too lucky and that a severe setback was inevitable. In this, the East Europeans seem similar to the South Koreans, who took their hardship in 1997–98 with the same surprising equanimity. After all, the average growth of Eastern Europe even including the crisis was 42 percent for the decade.

The Baltic states, in particular, which were new nations, remained concerned about their national sovereignty. They had been parts of the Russian or Soviet Empire for most of the time since the early 18th century, and they did not want to risk their independence again. They feared the financial crisis could undermine their sovereignty and stood up for their nations.[1]

The political economy of crisis differs greatly from that in ordinary times, and these nations knew how to handle crises. They had all undergone transition from socialism to capitalism, and all but Hungary had experienced severe inflationary crises after the end of communism. They also had experienced political crisis managers, whose careers revived when the crisis arrived, such as Lithuania's Prime Minister Andrius Kubilius, Latvia's Finance Minister Einars Repse, and Romania's omnipresent Mugur Isărescu. As the *Financial Times* put it: "The vicious 1990s post-Soviet slump made Latvians hardily resourceful."[2] Both people and leaders were prepared to do what was necessary.

The ideological wind was clearly liberal right-wing: favoring a somewhat purer market economy and a moderate retrenchment of the social welfare state. The Central and East European financial crisis is remarkable for everything that did not happen. There was no significant reaction against globalization, capitalism, the European Union, or the euro. The biggest losers were the irresponsible socialists in Hungary and the irresponsible oligarchs in Latvia. The big winners were the moderate center-right forces. The sensible Central and East European public wanted decisive action from their leaders to resolve their problems. This was reminiscent of the political economy of postcommunist transition, when radical reform and democracy went hand in hand.

Both ideology and organizations of the left had been severely weakened. In his book *The Rise and Decline of Nations*, Mancur Olson argued that countries that had suffered a major catastrophe, such as Germany and Japan during World War II, abandoned obsolete institutions that impeded

---

1. In 1994, Jacek Rostowski taught me that people do not care about financial stability on its own. The key to convincing them that financial stability is vital is to explain its significance for national sovereignty.

2. "The Lex Column: Greece/Latvia," *Financial Times*, May 7, 2010.

development and built new, better institutions.[3] In the same fashion, the new EU states had rid themselves of all obsolete institutions. Similarly, big capitalists were uncommonly weak after the old, big Soviet enterprises had collapsed.

The public and leaders in several of these countries stood remarkably firmly against devaluation. The political economy of devaluation seems to be poorly understood. The main capitalists, who are the biggest exporters, have the most to gain from devaluation, which would lead to greater income disparity. The majority of the population in the countries with fixed exchange rates preferred "internal devaluation" with wage cuts and deflation, presuming that their social cost would be less. Therefore, the currency boards of Estonia, Lithuania, and Bulgaria enjoyed amazing popularity and turned out to have many institutional strengths. They forced their governments to stay transparent and honest, especially checking their fiscal balance. Remarkably, Bulgaria, which the European Commission accused of being under the sway of organized crime, maintained a fiscal surplus until 2009.

The main opponents of radical fiscal adjustment, during both the postcommunist transition and the financial crisis, were the rent-seeking oligarchs or red entrepreneurs, typified by young communists who had made their money through dubious insider privatization or asset stripping—that is, seizing public enterprises or property by questionable means. Hungary, Romania, and Bulgaria suffered from the presence of big networks of more or less criminalized red entrepreneurs. Latvia had three oligarchs, who each controlled one center-right party and opposed fiscal tightening, while intermittently favoring devaluation.[4] As Joel Hellman noted on postcommunist transition, the main threat was not the people but the few rent-seeking winners. While they were the winners of postcommunist transition, these rent seekers appear the losers of the financial crisis.[5]

Most political scientists have perceived the fragmented parliamentary systems and their lack of stability as a problem, but these systems appear to have been beneficial for crisis resolution. In Hungary, one reformist socialist prime minister was replaced by a much more reformist socialist leader. Similarly, Latvia went through three center-right prime ministers, each more determined to resolve the crisis than his predecessor, like Winston Churchill replacing Neville Chamberlain as conservative British prime minister in 1940. East European politics would not have functioned

---

3. Mancur Olson, *The Rise and Decline of Nations* (New Haven: Yale University Press, 1982).

4. They were Aivars Lembergs (mayor of Ventspils), Andris Skele (former prime minister), and Ainars Slezers (former minister of transportation).

5. Joel Hellman, "Winners Take All: The Politics of Partial Reform in Postcommunist Transitions," *World Politics* 50, no. 2 (1998): 203–34.

so smoothly if these countries had had presidential systems with a president of a precrisis mind. These multiparty coalition governments adopted and carried out the radical public expenditure cuts and structural reforms that were necessary, proving their efficacy. The fragmentation was no obstacle but made more forceful policies possible. The least successful country has been Hungary, which stands out for having the greatest party consolidation and the most stable and long-lasting government.

Finally, the European Union had great and varied impact on its new member countries, which had acceded to the European Union in 2004 and 2007. In the 1990s, the candidate countries benefited from greater market access to the vast European market. As the accession process became serious, they were forced to adopt all the rules and regulations of the now 125,000 pages of legal text in the *acquis communautaire*. Most of it was beneficial improvement of legislation. As accession took place, a tremendous integration of trade and investment occurred, which contributed to high economic growth but also to the financial bubble. The Maastricht criteria or the Stability and Growth Pact were taken more seriously in the east than in the EU-15, since the easterners had to comply with the convergence criteria to be allowed to adopt the euro. The new East European EU members, the CEE-10, were stalwarts of EU standards.

These conclusions go against the grain of much of the academic writing on the political economy of reform, which has not stood this empirical test. First, it does not appear to be desirable to have a stable government in the midst of the crisis. On the contrary, a government that is perceived as the cause of trouble should be ousted as soon as possible. If its successor does not deliver, it should be sacked as well, or at least be disciplined by such a threat. Second, the worst form of stability is a steady presidential mandate. Therefore, a parliamentary system appears better suited to handle a severe crisis than a presidential one. Third, multiparty coalition governments seem more adept at handling severe crises than one-party majority governments (as in Hungary).

8

Eastern Europe and the Fiscal Crisis in the Eurozone

European leaders must act fast to contain the Greek crisis.
—Angela Merkel, May 7, 2010

The crisis resolution in Eastern Europe was close to ideal with its simple and clear logic. After two years of intensive care, these countries, the International Monetary Fund (IMF), and the European Commission could declare victory. But in the first half of 2010 a new financial crisis erupted in the eurozone, with multiple implications for Eastern Europe and its standing in the European Union.

The European Union is not a club of equals. Having expanded gradually, it is a two-tier club with old insiders roughly corresponding to the membership of the Economic and Monetary Union (EMU) and new outsiders, primarily Eastern Europe.[1] Especially France and Germany have repeatedly spoken about the need for a "two-speed" Europe, suggesting that the original six members of the European Union would integrate faster.[2] Ironically, the three big old members, France, Germany, and Italy, have stood out by doing the least reform, while Eastern Europe and the Nordic countries have done the most.

Instead, the EU core, whose exact composition has varied, has expropriated privileges for itself, not least in fiscal policy. EU fiscal policy is supposed to be ruled by the Maastricht criteria or the Stability and Growth Pact (SGP). But many countries grossly violated the Maastricht criteria on budget deficit and public debt (chapter 1). The original sin of the EMU was that both Belgium and Italy had entered with far too high public debt levels at the end of 1998, 117 and 115 percent of GDP, respectively, while

---

1. Of course, the United Kingdom, Denmark, and Sweden are not members of the eurozone, while Slovenia and Slovakia are.

2. They are France, Germany, Italy, Belgium, Netherlands, and Luxembourg.

the Greek debt was "only" 95 percent of GDP. Germany was just over the 60 percent ceiling and France just below. In 1998, Portugal, Spain, and Greece violated the budget ceiling of 3 percent of GDP. Germany exceeded the budget ceiling for the four years from 2002 to 2005 and France for three years. At the end of 2009, the average public debt of the EMU countries was a shocking 79 percent of GDP, and 10 of the 16 EMU countries but only two of the non-EMU countries (Hungary and the United Kingdom) exceeded the public debt ceiling.[3] Germany fulfilled the debt criterion only in 2000 and 2001, while France has not done so since 2002.

Most spectacular, in November 2003, Germany and France relinquished the little fiscal discipline that existed by jointly aborting the SGP, because they neglected to fulfill its criteria, but even so the ECOFIN Council (of the EU ministers of finance) decided to put the excessive deficit procedures for France and Germany on hold. The SGP was revised, so that a deficit above 3 percent of GDP was not necessarily considered excessive if it could be shown that the breach was "exceptional and temporary."[4] Since France and Germany openly jeopardized the SGP and received no penalty, it lost all credibility within the EMU, preparing the road to the current crisis. The problem was not the Maastricht criteria, which made a lot of sense, but the lack of implementation in the EMU.[5] As the *Economist* put it: "France and Germany led a rebellion against the disciplines of the 'stability and growth pact' on the first occasion it looked about to catch them. That signaled a free-for-all."[6] Fiscal standards were a joke within the EMU but they were taken seriously by EU members outside of the EMU.

When the financial crisis first hit, the eurozone countries also considered themselves immune to the IMF and its bailouts. However, when the crisis started to bite, they realized that they had to accept the same rules as others. The eurozone's fiscal crisis was far worse than the East European crisis, which was primarily a current account crisis. When the eurozone approached its crisis, the east had largely resolved its crisis and could inform the eurozone countries what to do. The eurozone crisis leveled Western Europe with Eastern Europe. The convergence of rules brought the new EU members closer to the old euro core, and institutions for the

---

3. The six virtuous countries were Cyprus, Finland, Luxembourg, Slovakia, Slovenia, and Spain—that is, three (Cyprus, Slovakia, and Slovenia) were recent additions, and only Spain was a large country.

4. José Manuel González-Páramo, "The Reform of the Stability and Growth Pact: An Assessment" (speech, conference on New Perspectives on Fiscal Sustainability, Frankfurt, October 13, 2005), available at www.ecb.int (accessed on May 15, 2010).

5. Jean Pisani-Ferry, "Euro-Area Governance: What Went Wrong? How to Repair It?" Bruegel Policy Contribution, Issue 2010/05 (Brussels: Bruegel, June 2010).

6. "Staring into the Abyss," *Economist*, July 10, 2010, 24.

European Union as a whole are likely to be strengthened. Yet as the eurozone accounts for most of Eastern Europe's exports, its crisis will slow down its recovery.

The Greek Tragedy

Greece was the worst fiscal sinner, having never complied with the Maastricht criteria. It joined the EMU in 2001, two years after the latter's creation. It violated the Maastricht rules persistently and blatantly. Spectacularly, Greece maintained an average budget deficit of 7.3 percent of GDP from 1990 to 2009, with a public debt never less than 94 percent of GDP. Its government was revealed to have repeatedly fudged its budget deficit.

Even so, Greece was never penalized. On the contrary, it was a major beneficiary of EU structural funds and farm subsidies, amounting to several percent of its GDP every year. Thanks to its membership in the EMU, Greece enjoyed almost as low yields as Germany on its treasury bills. Even so its production costs rose so that it became uncompetitive with a persistent large current account deficit and probably the least free economy within the European Union.

In early 2010, Southern Europe, or the so-called PIGS (Portugal, Italy, Greece, and Spain), was heading toward a serious fiscal crisis, with Greece in the lead. Greece's corrected budget deficit was 13.6 percent of GDP in 2009 and its public debt 115 percent of GDP. These revelations came in October 2009 after a newly elected socialist government under George Papandreou was sworn in. A first disclosure of the much larger budget deficit unleashed the crisis, and a second downward revision of the budget deficit in April 2010 eliminated all market confidence.

Rather than repeating the successful EU cooperation with the IMF in Eastern Europe, the EMU governments delayed crisis treatment, pursuing haphazard improvisations from February until May 2010, when financial markets exploded. The actors were the eurozone countries and the European Central Bank (ECB) rather than the European Union as a whole. Their policy line made little sense.

First, the other eurozone governments told Greece not to go to the IMF, denying it adequate professional and financial assistance. The Greek government listened to its EMU peers, even though their position had no legal basis. Michael Burda argued: "I doubt Europe could stomach giving away real authority on fiscal matters to a third party, especially given the dominant role of the US" in the IMF.[7] The rest of the world on the contrary complains that the IMF is excessively dominated by Europe-

---

7. Michael Burda, "Greece: It's Not All Tragedy," www.voxeu.org, March 13, 2010.

ans.[8] The IMF managing director has always been European (Frenchman Dominique Strauss-Kahn at the time) and the director for the European region was also European. The eurozone countries inevitably took on greater financial costs both by delaying action and by holding Greece away from the IMF. Moreover, the IMF is primarily financial and technocratic, which facilitates its role as crisis manager, whereas the European Union and the European governments are profoundly political, often making it more difficult for them to take principled decisions. Because the eurozone countries tried to take the lead, a vicious public dispute arose between Germany and Greece, which complicated the resolution of the Greek crisis.

Second, the eurozone countries denied Greece the right to an emergency loan, which all IMF members enjoy. The formal excuse was that Greece as a member of the EMU was supervised by the ECB. Article 125 of the Treaty on the Functioning of the European Union stipulates that neither the Union nor any member state could assume financial commitments of any other member state, prohibiting the European Commission and the ECB from providing financial support to a member state in financial hardship.[9] But accidents happen and each financial community needs adequate tools to handle them. This clause made the EMU dysfunctional and threatened its survival. Wolfgang Münchau commented: "Article 125 of the Lisbon treaty is the kind of law that is irrelevant until needed, at which point it becomes impossible to apply."[10]

Third, after leading Greece and themselves into a financial abyss by jeopardizing the SGP, the eurozone governments insisted on playing a guiding role in Greece, for which they had few qualifications and no institutions. The only justifications were really pride and privilege. German Finance Minister Wolfgang Schäuble endorsed a proposal to develop a European Monetary Fund,[11] but it was soon discarded.

Fourth, the European Union refused to deal with the cause of the financial crisis: fiscal malfunctioning of member governments. It avoided the topic of restoring the SGP. Instead, EU politicians were preoccupied with minor matters, such as the possible regulation of hedge funds,

---

8. My colleague Arvind Subramanian calls it the Euro-Atlantic Monetary Fund.

9. Treaty on the Functioning of the European Union, *Official Journal of the European Union*, Information and Notices C 115, volume 51, May 9, 2008, available at http://eur-lex.europa. eu.

10. Wolfgang Münchau, "Germany Pays for Merkel's Miscalculations," *Financial Times*, May 11, 2010.

11. "Schäuble liebäugelt mit einem EU-Währungsfonds [Schäuble Is Toying with an EU Monetary Fund]," *Die Welt am Sontag*, March 6, 2010; Daniel Gros and Thomas Mayer "Towards a Euro(pean) Monetary Fund," CEPS Policy Brief (Brussels: Centre for European Policy Studies, February 8, 2010)

private equity funds, and investment trusts through a new EU directive on alternative investment fund managers as well as the persecution of tax havens, and the German government restricted short-selling. None of these had contributed to the crisis. The Greek government responded by suggesting fiscal measures that were insufficient.

Münchau passed a harsh judgment: "Europe's leaders are not solving the problem, they are fighting a public relations war. Their target is not economic imbalances, but speculators: hedge funds, investment banks, bond market vigilantes and in particular, those ominous Anglo-Saxon rating agencies."[12] Similarly, some European leaders were preoccupied with "harmonization" of taxation and regulation, hindering structural reform. The main proponents of these arguments in spring 2010 were Germany, France, and the ECB.

However, the public and acrimonious debate as well as crisis in European financial markets helped to clear the thinking. Policymakers realized that their old positions were not viable. From May to July 2010, the same politicians were forced to reverse their thinking on all the key issues, and EU economic policy changed more than in the last decade since the launch of the euro, as often happens in financial crises.

The Greek Rescue Package of May 2, 2010

Finally, on May 2, 2010, the IMF was admitted to the center stage, as the ECB and the eurozone governments permitted the Greek government to call in the IMF as the agent of financial stabilization. The IMF and the European Union made an agreement with the Greek government on a standard IMF standby program for three years.

The Greek rulers became serious about fiscal policy. Substantial budget cuts were finally made. A first Greek stabilization program in March reduced the budget deficit by 4 percent of GDP in 2010. The IMF-EU standby program of May 2 demanded substantial additional spending cuts, raising the total cuts to 7.5 percent of GDP in 2010.

The no-bailout clause was circumvented. A stabilization program must be sufficiently financed, and the funding was unprecedented: credits of $145 billion (€110 billion), of which €80 billion from EU countries and €30 billion from the IMF, but nothing from any EU institution. Latvia's stabilization package, one-third of its GDP, would correspond to $100 billion for Greece, but since Greece's crisis was more severe, more funding was required. The IMF package corresponded to 32 times the Greek IMF quota, and the eurozone package for Greece to 0.9 percent of

---

12. Wolfgang Münchau, "The Eurozone Must Take Responsibility or It Will Split," *Financial Times*, May 10, 2010.

the eurozone's GDP. Since the eurozone countries had excluded everybody, they received neither sympathy nor financing, which was the price of their privilege.[13]

The question remained whether the Greek public debt of 115 percent of GDP or $400 billion was sustainable or needed to be restructured. The IMF program aimed to stabilize it at 140 percent of GDP in 2014, but with output likely to contract more than the IMF assumed, debt could easily rise above 150 percent of GDP. Greece was really an emerging market. Kenneth Rogoff noted "that most emerging markets run into trouble at external debt levels of merely 60 per cent of GDP" and "that a country can repay its debt does not necessarily mean it should choose to do so."[14] Barry Eichengreen put it in the affirmative: "Greece will restructure its debt... the only controversy is why a restructuring was not part of the initial IMF-EU rescue package."[15] As Rogoff and Carmen Reinhart have shown in their excellent history of financial crises, *This Time Is Different*, virtually all countries have at some time defaulted on their debt, even if they also argue that developed economies have graduated from defaults.[16]

Still Greece had no reason to abandon the euro. Not only would it lose its claim to European funding but also its departure from the euro would probably lead to a big depreciation, which could double its public debt in relation to its GDP, as the debt would be denominated in the then foreign currency, euro. Greece would default instantly on both public and most private debt, which would lead to total financial chaos.[17]

In effect, Greece was following the lead of the Baltic "internal devaluation," cutting public expenditures, wages, and pension obligations, while pursuing domestic structural reforms to reduce costs. The Baltic governments had shown the way by successfully insisting on the peg with strong popular support. A fixed exchange rate forces a country to reduce costs and undertake structural reform. This crisis can render Greece a freer and more competitive economy.

---

13. Slovakia, which had adopted the euro on January 1, 2009, changed government in June, and its new government refused to contribute.

14. Kenneth Rogoff, "Europe Finds that the Old Rules Still Apply," *Financial Times*, May 10, 2010.

15. Barry Eichengreen, "It Is Not Too Late for Europe," www.voxeu.org, May 7, 2010.

16. Carmen M. Reinhart and Kenneth S. Rogoff, *This Time Is Different: Eight Centuries of Financial Folly* (Princeton: Princeton University Press, 2009).

17. Marek Dabrowski, "Euro Crisis or Debt Crisis?" CASE Network E-briefs 9/2010 (Warsaw: Centre for Social and Economic Research, June 2010), www.case-research.eu.

The South European Rescue Package, May 9–10, 2010

The Greek rescue package was not sufficient to halt the spreading financial panic in Europe. Over the following week, fear of contagion spread to Portugal and Spain, as their bond yields rose and stock prices around the world plummeted. People spoke about a possible second Lehman Brothers shock.

The South European financial crisis illuminated the problem with both the European Union and the EMU: Europe is a halfway house. The long-awaited Lisbon Treaty had just come into force. It was being tested, and it was failing. The European Union had not obtained any more effective leadership or governance. Europe faced a clear-cut choice: to integrate with functioning fiscal policy coordination or to disintegrate.[18]

The cause of the Greek and South European financial crisis was not the Maastricht criteria but that they have never been imposed. The idea of a common European fiscal regime had hardly failed. On the contrary, the crisis showed how badly it was needed. The Scandinavian countries, the Netherlands, and Luxembourg had done well by sticking to the Maastricht criteria. So did the four EU currency board countries. The European Union's problem was its inability to discipline the core, the EMU, especially Germany and France, not the periphery, where new eastern EU members faced hard budget constraints and were forced to behave better than the core. By contrast, the privileged treatment of the PIGS, Belgium, France, and Germany had caused their severe public finance problems. Now, they were receiving the bill for their lack of fiscal discipline.

What a difference a week can make! After week-long financial panic, the EU ministers of finance held an extraordinary Council night session on May 9–10, making most of the necessary decisions.[19] This time it was the whole European Union, not just the EMU group.

Substantial financing was vital, and the European Union and the IMF put up nearly $1 trillion, consisting of €500 billion of EU funding and €250 billion of IMF funding.[20] The EU funding would consist of two parts. The bulk of €440 billion would be contributed by the EMU member states to a special purpose vehicle, to which Sweden and Poland volunteered to contribute as well. It was to be named the European Financial Stability Facility, designed as a temporary new EU institution. The remaining €60 billion would be added to the existing €50 billion balance-of-payments support fund, which had previously been reserved for non-eurozone EU

---

18. Wolfgang Münchau, "Europe's Choice Is to Integrate or Disintegrate," *Financial Times*, May 3, 2010.

19. Council of the European Union, "Extraordinary Council Meeting, Economic and Financial Affairs," press release 9/10, Brussels, May 2010.

20. Ibid.

members, and €14.6 billion had been committed to Hungary, Latvia, and Romania. It would be financed by all EU members. This complied with the first rule of financial crisis management, established by Walter Bagehot in *Lombard Street* (1873), that in a crisis loans should be granted to all comers on the basis of sound collateral "as largely as the public asks for them."[21]

Another improvement was the EU decision to accept bailouts. The European Council lifted its eyes to Article 122.2 in the Treaty of the Functioning of the European Union, which in no uncertain terms allowed bailouts:

> Where a Member State is in difficulties or is seriously threatened with severe difficulties caused by natural disasters or *exceptional occurrences beyond its control*, the Council, on a proposal from the Commission, may grant, under certain conditions, Union financial assistance to the Member State concerned [my emphasis].[22]

In order to enhance its credibility, the European Union once again invoked the authority of the IMF. The European Union also committed itself to strict fiscal policies and insisted on Portugal and Spain reducing their dangerously large public deficits. The ECB was allowed to carry out direct purchases of eurozone public and private debt to activate and restore frozen financial markets, as the US Federal Reserve had done from the fall of 2008. The European Union also activated a dollar swap line with the US Federal Reserve that had been agreed in the fall of 2008 but was allowed to lapse after that first rampant crisis was over.

Suddenly, the European Union had decided most of the necessary actions to resolve the financial crisis. The big outstanding questions were whether debt restructuring was necessary and how to police fiscal policy in the future.

East European Lessons Dawn on the Eurozone

The European Union suddenly found itself drawing lessons from what the East Europeans had done since the onset of the crisis in 2008. The central conclusion, as formulated by Martin Wolf, was: "As initially designed, the EMU has failed. It will succeed only if radically reformed."[23] The European Union and the ECB started doing just that.

First, the eurozone countries let the IMF lead in financial stabilization

---

21. Charles P. Kindleberger and Robert Aliber, *Manias, Panics, and Crashes*, 5th ed. (Hoboken, NJ: Wiley, 2005), 237.

22. Treaty on the Functioning of the European Union, *Official Journal of the European Union*, Information and Notices C 115, volume 51, May 9, 2008, available at http://eur-lex.europa.eu.

23. Martin Wolf, "Governments Up the Stakes in Their Fight with Markets," *Financial Times*, May 12, 2010.

and abandoned their prior ideas of the EMU's superiority and exceptionalism after the opposite had become evident. The IMF had the relevant competence and more credibility in handling financial emergencies than the ECB, the eurozone finance ministers, or the European Commission.

Second, the eurozone countries accepted once again that the fiscal discipline of the SGP was vital and that radical fiscal adjustment was possible and necessary. The corollary was that eurozone countries, such as Greece, were no longer so privileged that they could disregard EU rules. How the European Union is to impose fiscal discipline remains unclear, but during the crisis the bond market started enforcing the rules, by differentiating sharply between eurozone countries' bonds and punishing the fiscally weak countries with high bond yields.

Third, the eurozone abandoned the illogical no-bailout clause. A monetary union cannot survive severe financial crises without a fiscal rescue facility. Staring into the financial abyss, EU leaders recognized that they needed such facilities and made them sufficiently large. Essentially, the European Union decided to combine the monetary union with credible fiscal discipline and fiscal rescue funding. The distinction between first- and second-class members was blurred, and the European Union has become more equal. The ECB agreed to buy bonds and thus start participating in quantitative easing. Most of the bonds it bought were Greek government bonds.

The United States reengaged. It had minimized top-level engagement in the East European financial crisis and the South European financial crisis until the weekend of May 7–9, when top US policymakers engaged directly because they feared contagion to the United States and the rest of the world. Two major US tenets were that the financing had to be huge and the fiscal cuts credible. The United States accepted the sizable IMF intervention but did not offer bilateral assistance, though the US Federal Reserve revived swap credits to the ECB to make sure that it had sufficient dollar liquidity.[24]

The May 9–10 rescue operation was sufficient to stop financial panic and hinder contagion from the Greek crisis to Portugal and Spain. The Greek rescue package was so large that the country does not need to sell any bonds for about two years. The Greek debt service may not be sustainable, and a missing piece in the new European financial architecture is a system for sovereign debt restructuring within the EMU. Admittedly, debt restructuring is usually carried out ad hoc, but the European Union may benefit from an insolvency facility. It could be built on the new, but so far temporary, European Financial Stability Facility, which could become a European Monetary Fund, in the sense that it would be a fund for emergency bailouts of sovereign debt.

---

24. James Politi, "Fear of Contagion Drove US to Push for Action," *Financial Times*, May 11, 2010.

Following the example of the United States in May 2009, the European Union decided to carry out a bank stress test to quell worries about lacking transparency and insufficient capital in the banking system. The US stress test involved only 19 banks and the EU test 91 banks, but each covered 65 percent of the region's banking assets. The difference in the number of banks reflects the great concentration of the US banking system. The European stress test covered no fewer than 27 Spanish banks and 14 German banks but no more than six from the other EU countries, because Spain and Germany were the countries where the greatest problems were likely.[25] The result was published on July 23, 2010. The test did attain great transparency but appeared softer than the American one, and only seven small banks were considered to have too little capital. The required capital injection was only $4.5 billion compared with $75 billion in the US stress test.

An important consequence of the European bank stress test will be to bring the European Union closer together. Before the crisis, bank inspection had been strictly national, but the stress test was carried out by the EU Committee of European Banking Supervisors, which is a loose and newly formed institution pertaining to the European Commission. It applied to the EU-27 and was not reserved for the EMU of 16. The Committee of European Banking Supervisors was reinforced by the stress test and will soon become the European Banking Authority, an all-EU banking inspector, which was missing before the crisis but is now finally being set up. In parallel, similar all-European inspections for insurance and security markets are also being formed.

To most Europeans in the east and west, the euro remains attractive. If the euro had not existed, the European Union would probably have repeated its experience of competitive and disruptive devaluations of 1992, which gave the impetus to introduce the euro. Peter Sutherland formulates it starkly: "Without the single currency, Europe would be an economic wasteland. The cost of not having the euro would have been far greater over the past two years.... Competitive devaluations of national currencies after the financial crisis of 2008 would have led to economic chaos incomparably worse than the turbulence we are now experiencing."[26] The problem was not the euro per se but the inadequate governance structure. The smaller and more open an economy, the greater its inclination to peg to and eventually adopt the euro.

Through adequate U-turns, the European Union sorted out most of its financial policy problems in the second quarter of 2010. It allowed the IMF to take the lead in financial restoration also within the EMU. The

25. Committee of European Banking Supervisors, "CEBS's Statement on Key Features of the Extended EU-wide Stress Test," July 7, 2010, available at www.c-ebs.org (accessed on July 21, 2010).

26. Peter Sutherland, "Radical Reforms Can Save the Euro," *Financial Times*, June 30, 2010.

eurozone countries invited the rest of the European Union to commiserate about their financial problems. The SGP has been restored, and the bond market is likely to enforce it in the future. Together with the IMF, the European Union has succeeded in mobilizing sufficient bailout funds, and the European Union has time to contemplate what to do about sovereign insolvency.

For Eastern Europe, the EMU crisis in the spring of 2010 meant convergence with the EMU. The SGP applied not only to Eastern Europe but also to the eurozone. The IMF and the European Commission were now playing the same role for supervision of and emergency financing to both areas. To become more competitive eurozone countries were forced to carry out the structural reforms that the East Europeans had already undertaken in their internal devaluations. Eastern Europe is making its mark on the European Union with its lower public expenditures and taxes. In recent years, the European Union has seen personal income tax rates and corporate profit tax rates plummet because of tax competition from the east. In the regulatory sphere as well, competition is bringing down barriers, for example, in labor markets. The new EU-wide supervision of banks, security markets, and insurance offers new financial safeguards common to all EU members. The East Europeans have emerged as the successful pioneers of a new, more liberal, and fiscally responsible all-European economic system.

9

Toward European Convergence

Remember that time is money.
—Benjamin Franklin, 1748

Listening to French President Nicolas Sarkozy at the St. Petersburg International Economic Forum on June 19, 2010, I was struck by how social democratic this purported center-right politician sounded. But otherwise his line had changed. Rather than talking about the eurozone of 16 as usual, he spoke of the European Union of 27. The fiscal crisis in the eurozone offered the broader European Union, including its new eastern members, a seat at the common table.

Many policy lessons can be drawn from the East European financial crisis. At the time of this writing, the whole region is undergoing economic recovery, although the financial situation remains constrained in Hungary and Romania. The current threat to recovery is not primarily internal but external: the fiscal crisis in the eurozone, which is depressing recovery in Eastern Europe.

The cause of the crisis in Eastern Europe, as in East Asia in 1997, was large current account deficits in the private sector that had accumulated into large private foreign debt. The crisis was connected with pegged exchange rates, which attracted vast capital flows into these countries, leading to excessive monetary expansion and overheating, thus making them vulnerable to global disturbances. In East Asia's recovery, the East Asian tiger model proved sturdy, and East European capitalism appears similarly strong. But the lessons of this shock must be remembered in both Eastern Europe and the European Union as a whole.

Outcome of the Crisis in Eastern Europe

The most important outcome of the East European financial crisis was of course that the crisis was overcome fairly quickly. The main positive adjustment was a remarkably fast reduction of current account deficits, which swung to surpluses in the Baltic states, primarily because imports contracted more than exports. Central Europe achieved approximate balance, and Southeastern Europe reduced its deficits. International reserves rose in all the CEE-10 countries. In 2010, Latvia took only the cheap credits offered by the IMF and the European Commission but abstained from the more expensive bilateral emergency credits. Hungary even abstained from a couple of IMF disbursements. The exchange rates of Hungary and Romania recovered and stabilized. The remaining financial problems were large budget deficits and rising public debt, but only Hungary exceeded the Maastricht limit on government debt as before.

Inflation fell sharply so that all East European countries apart from Hungary and Romania now have less than 3 percent inflation. In spite of strains, the banking system survived with minimal losses at significant banks. No East European country was even close to sovereign default.

Carmen Reinhart and Kenneth Rogoff have argued that excessive leverage is always dangerous and that the form of indebtedness—private or public—does not matter much: "...sustained debt buildups (whether public, private or both) are important precursors to a financial crisis."[1] Yet, this point should not be taken too far. The real issue is to what extent the state will be forced to bail out the private sector, and the East European governments were quite successful in avoiding such compulsion. Apart from some recapitalization of state banks and subsidies to large state corporations, they minimized state aid, unlike Western Europe or the United States.

The most conspicuous negative outcome was substantial output declines, especially in the Baltic countries. Latvia saw a total decline in GDP of 25 percent, as the United States and Germany did during the Great Depression. Lithuania and Estonia were close behind with contractions of 17 and 18 percent, respectively, while the other countries had 4 to 8 percent of GDP decline, and Poland saw no reduction.

The other disturbing statistic is the rise in unemployment, which soared in four countries, the three Baltic countries and Slovakia. It seemed to have peaked in the first quarter of 2010 and then stabilized. Unemployment reached 20 percent in Latvia, 19 percent in Estonia, 17 percent in Lithuania, 15 percent in Slovakia, and 11 percent in Hungary. Yet, as a whole, unemployment has been less in Eastern Europe than in Western Europe. Slovenia, the Czech Republic, and Romania have had unemploy-

---

1. Carmen M. Reinhart and Kenneth S. Rogoff, *This Time Is Different: Eight Centuries of Financial Folly* (Princeton: Princeton University Press, 2009), 217.

Figure 9.1 Unemployment rate, monthly average, January 2008–June 2010

percent

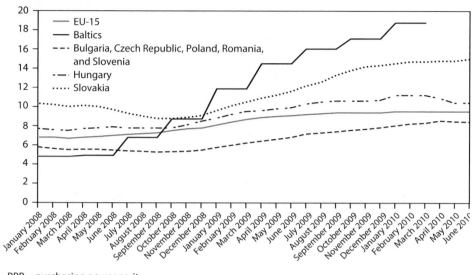

PPP = purchasing power parity

Note: GDP per capita in PPP (constant 2005 international dollars) as a share of average EU-15 GDP per capita in PPP.

Source: Eurostat database, http://epp.eurostat.ec.europa.eu (accessed on August 9, 2010).

ment peaking in the range of 7 to 8 percent, below the EU average, which reached a high of 9.6 percent, while Bulgaria and Poland have been close to that average. These five countries contain the vast majority of the East European population (figure 9.1). In comparison with Western Europe, unemployment in the east has risen less than output has fallen. The explanation is that the East European countries have more flexible labor markets and the worst-hit countries have seen substantial cuts in both public and private wages.

Fiscal policy was relatively straightforward. With the exception of Hungary, which never undertook a standard postcommunist fiscal adjustment, all the East European EU members had adopted decent fiscal policies before the crisis.[2] The Maastricht criteria had more impact on countries outside the Economic and Monetary Union (EMU) that wanted to adopt the euro early than on those that are already privileged members of the club. This coincides with standard club theory: A club is more effective in imposing its norms on a candidate for entry than in policing itself.

---

2. Admittedly, in 1995 Finance Minister Lajos Bokros attempted a serious fiscal stabilization, but it did not last long.

The European Union and the World Trade Organization are illustrative examples.

During the crisis, all CEE-10 countries in trouble cut public expenditures with great vigor. The three Baltic countries stood out: They slashed their budget deficits by 8 to 10 percent of GDP in 2009. These countries as well as others then forced structural changes, primarily in three neglected areas: public administration, health care, and education.

The tax systems in the whole region were already in good shape and were further improved with a broadening of tax bases as loopholes were eliminated. The low flat personal income taxes were maintained, as were the low corporate profit taxes, while value-added taxes and excise taxes were raised somewhat, and payroll taxes reduced. The big remaining reform in most countries concerns the pension system.

Constitutional rules have come to play a new, important role for economic policy during this crisis in two opposite ways. In Latvia and Romania, the constitutional courts refuted legislated reductions in pensions. As a consequence, pensioners have not shared the burden of austerity, and the share of pensions in GDP has risen sharply. Clearly, constitutions should not be allowed to block beneficial structural reforms, and if necessary such constitutions need to be amended. A new tendency is to limit public deficits or debts through the constitution. A recent amendment to the German constitution limits the budget deficit to 0.35 percent of GDP in 2016 and the Polish constitution restricts public debt to 55 percent of GDP. This new constitutional trend together with activist constitutional courts is likely to enhance austerity in the future.

The dominant role of 15 West European commercial banks in Eastern Europe greatly contributed to the development of the region's banking system before the financial crisis, but these banks were also the engines of the credit boom and overheating. Neither their domestic financial authorities nor East European bank supervision regulated them appropriately.[3] This observation raises the demand for pan-European regulation of multinational banks,[4] which the European Union is now acting on, with its establishment of the European Banking Authority and other bodies for supervision of insurance and security markets. Thus far, the West European banks have been reasonably helpful.

---

3. Bas B. Bakker and Anne-Marie Gulde, "The Credit Boom in the EU New Member States: Bad Luck or Bad Policies?" IMF Working Paper 10/130 (Washington: International Monetary Fund, 2010), 32; and a study of the regulation of Swedish banks in the Baltics showed that nobody felt responsible (personal communication with Swedish Member of Parliament and Professor Carl B. Hamilton on May 21, 2010).

4. Peter Zajc, "A Comparative Study of Bank Efficiency in Central and Eastern Europe: The Role of Foreign Ownership," *International Finance Review* 6 (2006): 117–56; Rainer Haselmann, "Strategies of Foreign Banks in Transition Economies," *Emerging Markets Review* 7, no. 4 (December 2006): 283–99.

The East European crisis also marked new collaboration between international players, primarily the IMF and the European Commission. The IMF successfully returned to the original Washington Consensus with relatively few conditions: a reasonable budget balance and a realistic exchange rate policy, while focusing more on bank restructuring. It provided far more money than previously, heeding Jeffrey Sachs's advice from the early 1990s.[5] By financing not only currency reserves but also large budget deficits, it has taken over much of the traditional subsidiary role of the World Bank. Its eventual success, however, depends on the political judgment of its management and major shareholders. The European Commission found its place with surprising ease as a partner of the IMF, following and controlling it while providing large financing.

EU Convergence or Divergence?

The most disputed issue was exchange rate policy, but curiously, no country has changed exchange rate policy during the crisis. The non-EMU countries in the CEE-10 insist on either currency boards or inflation targeting. The four currency board countries (Estonia, Latvia, Lithuania, and Bulgaria) are much more eager to adopt the euro. Their credibility, however, took a serious hit in the midst of the crisis. They had attracted too large funds, leading to excessive current account deficits and inflation. When global liquidity froze capital flew out fast. Still, these countries had a stellar fiscal record and soon they enhanced the credibility of their currency boards by standing firm. They deserve the euro and their euro adoption should be facilitated, as the IMF has argued.[6]

Since Europe is likely to face a deflationary environment for the next couple of years, it will be easier for the countries with currency boards to comply with the convergence criteria and adopt the euro now than before the crisis. The old problem, especially for the countries with currency boards, was excessive inflation, which raised an insurmountable hurdle and could not have been defeated without changing the monetary regime. Now fiscal contraction and other deflationary pressures have taken care of inflation. The remaining issue is to contain excessive fiscal deficits, which governments can and intend to do, and the crisis is giving them the democratic mandate to do so.

In the midst of the crisis, Estonia had quietly insisted on adopting the euro. After noticing that Estonia fulfilled the criteria on price stability, budget balance, public debt, and exchange rate stability, the European

---

5. Jeffrey D. Sachs, "Why Russia Has Failed to Stabilize," in *Russian Economic Reform at Risk,* ed. Anders Åslund (London: Pinter, 1995), 53–64.

6. Stefan Wagstyl, "Central and Eastern EU Nations Should Adopt Euro, Says IMF," *Financial Times,* April 6, 2009.

Commission concluded in its annual Convergence Report published on May 12, 2010, that "Estonia fulfils the conditions for the adoption of the euro."[7] On June 7, the eurozone's ministers of finance supported Estonia's application to adopt the euro, and the next day the ECOFIN Council agreed. On July 13, EU finance ministers made the final decision to keep the existing exchange rate to the euro. Estonia will introduce the euro on January 1, 2011. The governments of Bulgaria, Lithuania, and Latvia are determined to achieve a budget deficit of no more than 3 percent of GDP in 2012 in order to be allowed to adopt the euro in 2014. As Lithuanian Prime Minister Andrius Kubilius stated about the euro: "It's an instrument that will allow us to feel a little more safe in the global financial system."[8]

The countries with floating exchange rates are much less enthusiastic about adopting the euro. Their larger size also makes the euro adoption less urgent than for the small Baltic states. For them, the European Exchange Rate Mechanism (ERM II) exchange rate stability criterion requires that fluctuations be kept within the narrow band of +/−2.25 percent. An EMU candidate country can obtain permission from the European Commission and the ECB to revalue its central parity, as Slovakia did, but it cannot devalue.[9]

But the current ERM II rules make little sense. The European Union should consider a revision to offer a more sensible path to euro membership. First, the ERM II period of at least two years should be reduced, because it is destabilizing by encouraging too large capital inflows, as the experience of the Baltic countries has shown. The ERM II, with fixed exchange rates before euro adoption, is like telling a soldier in battle to walk slowly between the trenches to prove that he can withstand machine-gun fire. Second, at the very least a floor should be set for the inflation criterion to avoid the excessively harsh judgment the European Union passed on Lithuania's inflation in 2006 or demand deflation. As Zsolt Darvas and Jean Pisani-Ferry have argued, a minimum threshold for inflation for euro candidate countries should be set. A limit of 2 percent—the ECB inflation target—seems appropriate, while the current rules set it at 1 percent (that is, 1.5 percentage points above the average of the three lowest inflation rates among the 27 EU countries).[10] The various inflation-targeting central banks have either 2 or 3 percent inflation as their target, and under-

7. European Commission, "Convergence Report 2010," *European Economy* 3 (provisional edition, Brussels, 2010), 11–14.

8. Paul Hannon, "Why Lithuania Still Wants to Adopt the Euro," *Wall Street Journal Europe*, June 23, 2010.

9. I owe this point to Marek Dabrowski.

10. Zsolt Darvas and Jean Pisani-Ferry, "Avoiding a New European Divide," Bruegel Policy Brief no. 10 (Brussels: Bruegel, December 2008). Several countries currently have deflation.

shooting would not be beneficial. Third, ERM II countries should be given ample access to credit swaps if need arises again.[11]

Only in recent years has inflation targeting worked well in Poland and the Czech Republic, and exchange rate volatility has been scary during the crisis. The fiscal softness of Hungary and Romania undermines the case for inflation targeting, though it was much purer in Poland and the Czech Republic. Jiri Jonas and Frederic Mishkin have pointed out: "Even after EU accession, inflation targeting can remain the main pillar of monetary strategy...."[12] It should be favored until an EU country can actually adopt the euro.

In this financial crisis, the euro proved credible both in countries that had adopted it officially (Slovenia and Slovakia) and unilaterally (Kosovo and Montenegro). Paradoxically, currency traders perceived the monetary regimes of Kosovo and Montenegro as more credible than those of the virtuous Baltic countries. The euro on its own has greater credibility than the ECB. So much for the ERM II! The conclusion is once again that the expansion of the EMU should be facilitated and the ERM II abridged.

Stephen Roach has succinctly summarized the causes of the East Asian crisis of 1997–98: "That crisis stemmed largely from Asia's vulnerability to the vicissitudes of international capital flows. Lacking in foreign exchange reserves, overly exposed to short-term external debt and with rigid currency pegs, the region stood little chance when the hot money started to flee."[13] A lesson for the EU countries outside the EMU is that they cannot rely on the ECB or the European Union but need to hold sufficient international reserves themselves.

No government should accept major currency mismatches, that is, large domestic loans in foreign currency, especially not to consumers, and they can be regulated away.[14] But in June 2010, an ordinary Polish citizen could obtain a euro mortgage fixed for 30 years for as little as 3 percent a year, while a zloty mortgage cost 6 percent a year.[15] Bank regulation

11. Jean Pisani-Ferry and Adam S. Posen, eds., *The Euro at Ten: The Next Global Currency?* (Washington: Peterson Institute for International Economics, 2009), 13; Zsolt Darvas and György Szapáry, "Euro Area Enlargement and Euro Adoption Strategies," *European Economy*, Economic Papers 304 (Brussels: European Union, February 2008); Darvas and Pisani-Ferry, "Avoiding a New European Divide."

12. Jiri Jonas and Frederic S. Mishkin, "Inflation Targeting in Transition Economies: Experience and Prospects," in *The Inflation Targeting Debate*, eds. Ben S. Bernanke and Michael Woodford (Chicago: University of Chicago Press for the National Bureau of Economic Research, 2005): 410.

13. Stephen Roach, "The New Lesson for Resilient Asia," *Financial Times*, June 9, 2010.

14. Morris Goldstein and Philip Turner, *Controlling Currency Mismatches in Emerging Markets* (Washington: Institute for International Economics, 2004); Morris Goldstein, "Emerging-Market Financial Crises: Lessons and Prospects" (speech at the 2007 Annual Meeting, Institute of International Finance, Washington, October 20, 2007).

15. Personal communication with such a borrower in Warsaw on June 7, 2010.

can mitigate this market distortion, but outright prohibition of foreign currency loans is unrealistic in a small open market economy.

The most controversial issues are connected with the ECB: its monetary policy, the expansion of the euro, and exchange rate policy before adoption of the euro. The ECB widened the divide between the EMU and neighboring countries through its generosity to the free-riding insiders and its stinginess to EU outsiders in the early stage of the crisis.[16] Especially disturbing is that the ECB did nothing to help the virtuous countries with currency boards. If the ECB had provided swap loans to the Baltic states, Poland, and the Czech Republic, by accepting government bonds denominated in local currencies of non-eurozone EU countries as collateral, as Darvas and Pisani-Ferry advocated, the Baltic financial crisis would in all probability have been contained.[17] Neither before, during, nor after the crisis did the ECB undertake any action to promote financial stability in the EU countries outside the EMU. Through its spectacular inaction, not recognizing any regional responsibility, the ECB has earned a black eye. The rest of the world has been left wondering about its competence to manage European monetary affairs. As Pisani-Ferry and Adam S. Posen write:

> ...the euro did little to improve the crisis response of neighboring countries in Central and Eastern Europe.... Even if the formal mandates of the [ECB] and the Eurogroup...do not formally include it, broader stability in the region should be a major economic and political objective as well.[18]

Posen continues:

> The global financial crisis has if anything clearly displayed the geopolitical limitations on the euro's global role because the euro area authorities have failed to show leadership even as a regional anchor currency. A successful regional currency role for the euro would entail fulfilling responsibilities toward countries in the region that have adopted the euro as a monetary anchor or whose financial systems are partially euroized.[19]

Two big policy questions going forward are how and how fast to expand the euro. The crisis has proven the extreme danger of not having access to ECB liquidity. The risk of overheating due to free capital flows and excessive inflation in countries on the EU periphery remains, but

---

16. Darvas and Pisani-Ferry, "Avoiding a New European Divide."

17. Zsolt Darvas and Jean Pisani-Ferry, "Eastern European Currencies Need Help Now," *Wall Street Journal*, March 12, 2009.

18. Pisani-Ferry and Posen, eds., *The Euro at Ten: The Next Global Currency*, 5.

19. Adam S. Posen, "Geopolitical Limits of the Euro's Global Role," in *The Euro at Ten: The Next Global Currency?* eds. Jean Pisani-Ferry and Adam Posen (Washington: Peterson Institute for International Economics, 2009), 93.

presumably it will be much smaller for the next decade because of the recent financial crisis, which will limit credit expansion for years to come as banks deleverage.

The logical conclusion of Eastern Europe's suffering from the excesses of the eurozone governments and the ECB's loose monetary policy is of course that they demand rights as EU members and co-owners of the ECB to control both fiscal policies of the eurozone countries and the monetary policy of the ECB. Their influence on EU financial policy will be reinforced as they will gain seats in the new EU-wide financial supervision agencies that are supposed to improve inter-European bank, insurance, and security-market inspection.

The Last Shall Be the First

The current European financial crisis is reminiscent of the so-called Foundation Crisis (*Gründerkrise*) in Germany in 1873 after the jubilation over German unification. In a similar fashion, most EMU countries abandoned agreed fiscal constraints and the ECB flooded Europe with ample credit that went into asset speculation, and a typical bust followed, as Margrit Grabas has argued.[20] Europe would hardly have been hit by such a severe financial crisis if the EMU had not been established, because the old Bundesbank would have insisted on its old strict monetary policy and other countries would have been forced to follow, but the exchange rate chaos of 1992 would probably have been repeated.

The German Foundation Crisis was followed by two decades of deleveraging and slower economic growth from 1874 to 1896.[21] Today, long-term deleveraging appears inevitable, and the question is to what extent it will be undertaken through budget cuts, inflation, debt restructuring, or debt-equity swaps. With less credit available, savings and bank deposits will probably rise, which should render the banking systems in Eastern Europe more stable. Presumably, the East European countries will also aim at keeping larger precautionary currency reserves in the future. These factors will contribute to financial stability, but growth is likely to be significantly lower for the next decade.

Few things are as beneficial for progress as a total and complete humiliation, which the recent European financial debacle has been. It is a good reason for Europeans to straighten their thinking. The first big

20. Margrit Grabas, "Die Gründerkrise von 1873/79–Jähes Ende liberaler Blütenträume. Eine konjunkturhistorische Betrachtung vor dem Hintergrund der Globalisierungsrezession von 2008/2009," *Internationale Wissenschaftliche Vereinigung Weltwirtschaft und Weltpolitik (IWVWW)* nos. 182/183 (2009), 66–82.

21. Walt W. Rostow, *The World Economy: History and Prospect* (Austin: University of Texas Press, 1978).

lesson from the East European crisis concerns exchange rate policy. The greatest surprise was that the worst-hit countries—Latvia, Lithuania, and Estonia—were not forced to devalue, contrary to the claims of a broad chorus of American economists. Instead, these three Baltic countries pursued what they called "internal devaluation." Their governments cut public wages by up to 35 percent, and the private sector followed suit. They slashed public expenditures and their cost levels became competitive, allowing them to turn their large current account deficits swiftly to substantial surpluses. Both inflation targeting and pegs remain viable exchange rate policies, and internal devaluation is likely to become the rule for EMU countries in financial hardship.

Second, the East European crisis offers clear insights into the political economy of crisis. When the going gets tough, politics become a pragmatic matter of solving vital problems, while rational expectations with tradeoffs between various social groups are no longer politically relevant. Instead of widely predicted social unrest, the East European public has accepted their hardship with minimal protests. After many years of high economic growth, people were prepared for some suffering. These states had recently become free and were ready to stand up for their nations, and they were used to crisis from the postcommunist transition. Most crisis countries changed governments during the crisis and some of them twice, and the new governments were generally more determined and competent in their crisis policies, showing that frequent government changes may be beneficial for crisis resolution. Eastern Europe's fragmented proportional parliaments did not hinder crisis resolution but on the contrary made it possible to swiftly change governments when the incumbents fell short. They do not need to wait for an ordinary presidential election to get a competent government. Frequent government changes have facilitated the selection of more able leaders, who promoted more resolute anticrisis policies. The most successful governments were coalition governments of several parties, running counter to frequent views among political scientists that political stability, strong parties, and a powerful executive are beneficial. Many complain about the lack of leadership in Europe, but Eastern Europe has many eminent leaders. The current Baltic prime ministers stand out. For leadership, the European Union would be well advised to look to the east.

Third, a new European fiscal retrenchment is being carried out on the basis of a new political economy of pragmatism and fiscal conservatism. The center-right has never been stronger in Eastern Europe. Conspicuously, no reaction against capitalism or globalization has been apparent. Nobody is talking about capital controls. East European citizens blamed corruption and irresponsibility at home for their misfortunes, which were often associated with former communists. The fiscal balance can be restored only through vigorous cuts in public expenditures. Therefore, the large government redistribution in Europe, which in particular Vito Tanzi has long exposed, is now being addressed and is likely to be reduced.[22] The lesson from the East European crisis is that it is politically possible to cut public expenditures, salaries, and employment, as well as rationalize health care and education. The big remaining task is pension reform. The tax reforms in Eastern Europe with low flat income taxes and similarly low corporate taxes are surviving. The Stability and Growth Pact is being reinforced, since people and politicians have recognized the depth of the fiscal crisis. The postcommunist crisis forced the East European economic systems to be leaner and more efficient. This crisis is likely to persuade the West Europeans to do the same. Europe is moving toward a more efficient economic model without forgetting social values.

Fourth, the IMF stands out as the great victor on the international stage. It revived the old Washington Consensus of a few rudimentary financial conditions, such as tenable exchange rate policy and reasonable fiscal and monetary policy, but it allowed the well-governed countries larger public deficits during the crisis and offered much more financing, also for budgets, than before with the understanding that this was a temporary current account crisis. It acted faster than usual. The European Commission entered into an astonishingly successful partnership with the IMF in Eastern Europe. It allowed the IMF to take the lead, while providing substantial financing, more than the IMF in the case of Latvia, and it checked the work of the IMF. When financial crisis hit the euro area, however, the European Union seemed to have forgotten all its fortuitous lessons from Eastern Europe, attempting to keep the IMF out. In the end, the European Union came to its senses and let the IMF take the lead also within the eurozone, which helped mitigate the crisis.

Fifth, the ECB has been the great disappointment in the East European financial crisis. Its single contribution was to expand its credit supply to salvage the European banking system in the fall of 2008, also saving their subsidiaries in Eastern Europe. Before the crisis, however, the ECB ignored financial stability and the massive overheating in some EU members both inside and outside the euro area. The entry conditions to the eurozone demand that a country peg its exchange rate to the euro for at least two years, but the ECB did nothing to stabilize the economies of these euro candidate countries. It could have offered swap credits to eastern EU economies outside the euro area, but it did not. Evidently, the ECB needs to reconsider its policies, especially outside the eurozone, and become more proactive.

In the end, this crisis is likely to benefit both Eastern and Western Europe and thus the European Union. Western Europe will have to learn from Eastern Europe, thus erasing the current division between first- and second-class members in the European Union. The East Euro-

---

22. Vito Tanzi and Ludger Schuknecht, *Public Spending in the 20th Century* (Cambridge: Cambridge University Press, 2000).

pean countries have persistently had much higher growth rates than the West European countries, and economic convergence between them in terms of GDP per capita has been impressive for the last 18 years. Thanks to the East Europeans, the West Europeans have slashed their corporate profit tax rates and have also been enticed to liberalize their labor markets. Now, they will also learn fiscal policy from the east. Rather than being the laggards, the East Europeans will be the leaders in economic policymaking.

All this amounts to convergence rather than divergence. Thus the title of this book: *The Last Shall Be the First.*[23]

---

23. I owe this title to a suggestion from my colleague Adam S. Posen.

Index

ECB. *See* European Central Bank
ECOFIN Council, 9, 10, 80, 92, 108
Economic and Monetary Union (EMU), 32
  eurozone crisis and, 91–92
  Greek crisis and, 93
  interest rates determined by, 55
  membership, 4*t*, 8, 35, 101
  money supply, 18
  South European crisis and, 97–98
economic convergence reports, 9, 57–58,
    107–108
economic growth, 1, 4*t*
  after crisis resolution, 48, 49*f*, 104
  current account deficit and, 16, 17*f*
  exchange rate policy and, 59, 65
  during postcommunist transition, 14–16,
    15*f*, 88
economic policy. *See* fiscal policy
economic reform, 13
EIB (European Investment Bank), 7, 33,
    71–73, 83
EMU. *See* Economic and Monetary Union
ERM II (European Exchange Rate
    Mechanism), 8–9, 55, 79, 108–109
Erste (Austria), 68
eruption of crisis, 25–29
Estonia
  convergence report, 107–108
  crisis resolution, 41–42
  euro adoption, 58
  housing prices, 21
  overview of, 4*t*–5*t*
  politics, 41
euro adoption, 8–10, 54
  criteria for, 79
  by Lithuania, 57–58
  outcome of crisis and, 107–109
euro overvaluation, 28
European Bank Coordination Initiative
    (Vienna Initiative), 71–72
European Bank for Reconstruction and
    Development (EBRD), 6–7, 33, 71–73,
    82–83
European Banking Authority, 100, 106
European Central Bank (ECB), 6, 18, 43
  Baltic exchange rate policy and, 57
  Greek crisis and, 93, 95
  monetary policy, 53, 66, 110–11
  outcome of crisis and, 110, 113
  role of, 78–80, 83, 99, 110, 113
  South European rescue package, 98
European Commission
  balance-of-payments support facility, 78
  Baltic exchange rate policy and, 57

  role of, 83, 107, 113
  support for IMF standby programs, 6–7,
    32–33, 38
  Vienna Initiative, 71–73
European Council, 58
  bailout policy, 98, 99
  balance-of-payments support facility, 78
European Exchange Rate Mechanism (ERM
    II), 8–9, 55, 79, 108–109
European Financial Stability Facility, 97, 99
European Investment Bank (EIB), 7, 33,
    71–73, 83
European Monetary Fund, 94, 99
European Monetary System collapse (1992),
    65
European Parliament, 85
European Union
  bank stress test, 100
  convergence criteria, 9, 57–58, 107–11
  fiscal policy, 91–92, 99
  Greek crisis and, 93–95, 99
  Latvian assistance, 38
  membership, 4*t*, 8, 13–14, 24
  role of, 77–78, 83, 90, 101
  South European crisis and, 97–98
  support for IMF, 76, 78
eurozone
  crisis management within, 8, 100–101, 113
  current account flows in, 2
  fiscal crisis in, 91–101, 103
  Greek crisis and, 93–96
  lessons learned, 98–101, 110–14
  members of, 8
excessive deficit procedures, 10
exchange rate policy. *See also specific policy*
  available options, 65–66
  budget deficits and, 56, 57*f*
  CEE-10 grouped by, 3*b*, 4*t*, 5–6, 54
  credit crunch and, 27–28
  currency reserves and, 18
  dilemma created by, 12, 53–66
  economic growth and, 59, 65
  ERM II, 8–9, 55, 79, 108–109
  Greek crisis and, 96
  IMF, 65–66, 77
  outcome of crisis and, 107–12
  overheating and, 16, 21–22, 32, 58–59
export demand, economic growth driven
    by, 16

FDI. *See* foreign direct investment
FIDESZ (Alliance of Young Democrats), 33
Finland, 77
fiscal adjustment programs. *See* crisis
    resolution

Other Publications from the Peterson Institute for International Economics

WORKING PAPERS

* = out of print

POLICY ANALYSES IN INTERNATIONAL ECONOMICS Series

WORKS IN PROGRESS

DISTRIBUTORS OUTSIDE THE UNITED STATES

Australia, New Zealand,
and Papua New Guinea
D. A. Information Services
648 Whitehorse Road
Mitcham, Victoria 3132, Australia
Tel: 61-3-9210-7777
Fax: 61-3-9210-7788
Email: service@dadirect.com.au
www.dadirect.com.au

India, Bangladesh, Nepal, and Sri Lanka
Viva Books Private Limited
Mr. Vinod Vasishtha
4737/23 Ansari Road
Daryaganj, New Delhi 110002
India
Tel: 91-11-4224-2200
Fax: 91-11-4224-2240
Email: viva@vivagroupindia.net
www.vivagroupindia.com

Mexico, Central America, South America,
and Puerto Rico
US PubRep, Inc.
311 Dean Drive
Rockville, MD 20851
Tel: 301-838-9276
Fax: 301-838-9278
Email: c.falk@ieee.org

Asia (*Brunei, Burma, Cambodia, China,*
Hong Kong, Indonesia, Korea, Laos, Malaysia,
Philippines, Singapore, Taiwan, Thailand,
and Vietnam)
East-West Export Books (EWEB)
University of Hawaii Press
2840 Kolowalu Street
Honolulu, Hawaii 96822-1888
Tel: 808-956-8830
Fax: 808-988-6052
Email: eweb@hawaii.edu

Canada
Renouf Bookstore
5369 Canotek Road, Unit 1
Ottawa, Ontario KlJ 9J3, Canada
Tel: 613-745-2665
Fax: 613-745-7660
www.renoufbooks.com

Japan
United Publishers Services Ltd.
1-32-5, Higashi-shinagawa
Shinagawa-ku, Tokyo 140-0002
Japan
Tel: 81-3-5479-7251
Fax: 81-3-5479-7307
Email: purchasing@ups.co.jp
For trade accounts only. Individuals will find
Institute books in leading Tokyo bookstores.

Middle East
MERIC
2 Bahgat Ali Street, El Masry Towers
Tower D, Apt. 24
Zamalek, Cairo
Egypt
Tel. 20-2-7633824
Fax: 20-2-7369355
Email: mahmoud_fouda@mericonline.com
www.mericonline.com

United Kingdom, Europe
(*including Russia and Turkey*), **Africa,**
and Israel
The Eurospan Group
c/o Turpin Distribution
Pegasus Drive
Stratton Business Park
Biggleswade, Bedfordshire
SG18 8TQ
United Kingdom
Tel: 44 (0) 1767-604972
Fax: 44 (0) 1767-601640
Email: eurospan@turpin-distribution.com
www.eurospangroup.com/bookstore

Visit our website at:
www.piie.com
E-mail orders to:
petersonmail@presswarehouse.com